What Christian leaders are saying about this book .

D1605829

"Any sustained move of God will require a wedding of both passion and strategy; a joint congress of the visionary and the practical. I commend Ralph in this confronting book. He is onto something. There can be a bridge laid between Boomers and Busters. And if we can get our egos out of the way, that bridge can become a turnpike to the future of the church. This book is a part of that bridge."

Gary Goodell
Pastor, Vineyard Christian Fellowship
San Diego, California

"I know no one more *sensitive* to the challenge of contemporary evangelism, or more *sensible* in developing a valid means of response to the hurts and hopes of today's generation than Ralph Moore. I heartily recommend our attention to this work."

Jack Hayford
Pastor, Church on the Way
Van Nuys, California

"This is a book that stimulates the mind, challenges the heart, and causes the soul and spirit to seek after God until we find Him and know Him as He really is."

Don Long
General Supervisor, International Foursquare Church
Los Angeles, California

"I've watched Ralph Moore's life and ministry for three decades and know few leaders more qualified to speak to the Church about revival, church planting, and evangelism. Ralph has a way of tenderly exposing the cracks in the rim of your evangelism philosophy. His work has caused me to look close at my approach to evangelism. This should be a textbook for all those who seek to minister the love of God to a lost world."

Ron Mehl
Pastor, Beaverton Foursquare Church
Beaverton, Oregon
Author of *God Works the Night Shift* and
Meeting God at a Dead End

"Moore's statement, 'Reproducing ourselves in others and multiplying the church seems the highest calling for any life' is fulfilled in the life of the author."

Marlin Mull
General Director, Evangelism and Church Growth
Wesleyan Churches

"Will the church be able to connect with a new generation in a post-Christian age? Ralph Moore has written the right book for the right time!"

Michael Slaughter
Pastor, Ohio United Methodist Church
Ginghamsburg, Ohio
Author of *Spiritual Entrepreneurs*

"Few doubt that God has a special plan for America. But few have been given the creative insights into what is really happening that Ralph Moore shares in this book. *Friends* gives us a fresh and dynamic look at the good, the bad, and the unlimited future possibilities of our nation."

C. Peter Wagner
Dean, Fuller Theological Seminary
Colorado Campus

Friends:
How to Evangelize Generation X

RALPH MOORE

◢ STRAIGHT STREET PUBLISHING
Honolulu, Hawaii

◤ STRAIGHT STREET PUBLISHING

Oahu • Hawaii

For information, contact:
Straight Street Publishing
P.O. Box 240041
Honolulu, HI 96824-0041
   Phone (800) 711-9369 toll-free
   Fax (808) 247-2070

Unless otherwise indicated, all Scripture quotations are taken from the *Holy Bible,* New Living Translation, copyright ©1996. Used by permission of Tyndale House Publishers, Inc., Wheaton, Illinois 60189. All rights reserved. Scriptures marked (KJV) are taken from the *Holy Bible,* King James Version.

Book design by Darlene O.S. Ching
Cover design by Jan Avellana

Edited by:
Darlene O.S. Ching, Wendell Elento, and Colleen Itano

Library of Congress Cataloging-in-Publication Data

   Moore, Ralph
   Friends: How to Evangelize Generation X / Ralph Moore
        p.   cm.
        Includes references
        ISBN 0-9628127-6-5
        1. Church work with young adults.
        2. Generation X — Religious life.
        3. Evangelistic work.   4. Evangelicalism.
        I. Title.
        BV4446.M66 1997   259.23-dc20

Printed in the United States of America.
   98 99 00 01   10 9 8 7 6 5 4 3 2

Contents

Acknowledgments 7

Preface 9

Section I: Anticipating an Awakening

1. Renewal, Revival or Awakening? 15
2. A Generational Imperative 21
3. Morals, Mores and More 31

Section II: Understanding Rising Movements

4. Mechanics of Revival 41
5. Fires of Personal Evangelism 49
6. Embracing Revival 57

Section III: Moving the Harvest Into Barns

7. Moving the Harvest Into Barns 65

Section IV: Shifting Our Paradigms

8. Rethinking Our Churches 75
9. Rethinking Education 81

Section V: Labor for the Harvest

10. Church Planting in America's Revivals   93
11. From Laymen to Pastors   105
12. Locally-Reproduced Leaders   113

Section VI: Facing Tomorrow

13. A Message to Boomers   125
14. Authenticity   137
15. Building Bridges   151
16. Managing Generation X   165
17. Churches for Generation X   177
18. Another Perspective on Evangelism   193
19. Weighing the Options   207

Endnotes   211

Acknowledgments

To Carl and Kelly, the Xers who taught me the most. Also, thanks to Justin, Tom-Tom, Brandon, Amber, Dana, Julie and Gibo. You all stretched my wineskin with your hard questions, unquestionable love, and crazy antics. Finally, thanks to my wonderful wife, Ruby. Your support and flexibility keep us all going.

Preface

This book is intended to do three things:

1. Motivate church leaders to understand that our future depends on our success (or lack of it) with Generation X and to give Xers a higher priority on their personal and institutional agendas.

2. Press for relationship building as opposed to the tendency to try to reach this generation through new programs.

3. Provide some of the tools necessary to do the job.

Difficult to evangelize and overlooked by church leaders, this group is sliding past the years when most people commit their lives to Christ. Evangelism is easiest when the target audience is in their teens, slightly more difficult for 20-somethings, and a painful task after that. Their rate of evangelism is just 57 percent that of the Baby Boomers at this stage of life. Fortunately, the Christian media is waking to the need to reach Generation X. Unfortunately, we've "discovered" the Millennial generation at just about the same time. The danger is that we will altogether skip the Xers in favor of their younger siblings.

"Friends" is more than a take-off on the name of the TV show. It points to the defining characteristic of Generation X. They are simply better at relationships than the two generations that preceded them. They prioritize their time around relationships. They despise divorce. They are skeptical of the institutions and materialistic systems that led them to inherit a debt-laden, divorce-riddled society. They apply that skepticism to the church. Their doubts preclude any institutional approach to winning them. They are, however, wonderfully open to friendships that cross generational boundaries. While we may not be able to organize our way to success, we might get there by drinking espresso or eating pizza with a few Xers.

This book was born about a decade ago when our very successful high school ministry began graduating seniors who wanted nothing to do with our equally-inviting singles ministry. The concepts gained strength when my own kids moved to the mainland, but held onto their network of local friends in ways that I never dreamed of when I left home. The manuscript then stood up and screamed, "Write me!" when seven young people began searching for answers "about God" in my living room on Thursday evenings. It finally flowed onto paper when I began sharing what I was learning with fellow pastors and at leadership seminars. The material moved at least one denomination to focus on Generation X, and another is scratching its head trying to regain its evangelistic zeal for young people. My own congregation now boasts more Xers than any other adult generation.

Hopefully, this book will aid you in your desire to fulfill the Great Commission in this generation.

Ultimately, the task is spiritual. We can study current sociology and the history of revival and still miss the point. The "how-to" books are soon to follow. I stepped away from a major publisher who asked me to turn this into a "how-to" manual. The purpose of this book does not include mechanics. At this point, we would do best to realize our need to sit down with a few Gen Xers and ask them what they think of our ministry. We need to learn what they want and need. If two or more of us get together in *His* name, we can count on Him to be in our midst. He will lead us down the path we must walk. Maybe, after hanging around with the Lord and some potential young leaders, He will give you the insight to bless the rest of us with a "how-to" book based on your victories.

This book was written in a spirit of submission to all who read it. I pray that I don't sound strident or pushy. I trust that something good comes out of you and I spending the next few hours together, sharing words and ideas. My earnest desire is simply that our lives are not in vain.

Ralph Moore
Kaneohe, Hawaii
www.hopechapel.com

Section I

Anticipating an Awakening

1

Renewal, Revival or Awakening?

Drug dealers became street evangelists. Topless dancers transformed into Sunday school teachers. Churches sprang up in warehouses, old movie theaters and on public beaches. The late 1960s and early 1970s were a time of spiritual realignment for my own generation.

I entered pastoral ministry during an earthquaking return to Christianity. The whole culture reawakened to the possibility of a God who cared about the affairs of men. Not everyone was converted. America did not become a Christian nation. But the movement was strong enough that a United States president was elected largely on the strength of his testimony as a "born-again Christian."

Our church was alive with enthusiasm. People came to the Lord daily. Virtually every decision we made bore fruit for the harvest. Later, as the move of God began to wane, I was thrust into a search for the match that might rekindle such a fire. We all know that match is prayer, but exactly what are we praying for? How high are we to set our sights? The Scriptures promise that God will hear prayers and heal the land whenever His people humble themselves and pray, turning from their own wickedness.[1] Renewal, revival or awakening? Which should we be praying for? Aren't they all synonyms? What earthshaking importance is there in the choice of a word? In this case, a great deal. The choice of words becomes a determinate of behavior as well as a prayer target. We will probably get whatever we envision as we seek the Lord for His blessings on ourselves, our churches and our culture.

Renewal

A renewal is a time of refreshing in a church or an individual believer. The assumption is that life still exists but needs a little refreshing. A friend recently chided me for always talking about revival. He said the very word seems to put off the responsibility for continually renewing our walk with the Lord and the spiritual life of our churches. His suggestion is that we will gain more if we limit our thinking to the concept of self renewal by following the disciplines of the Spirit.

Revival

My friend is right and wrong at the same time. True enough, renewal is the responsibility of every Christian and certainly of every pastor. But we live in an age of decay. Liberal churches often forsake the teaching of Scripture for a religious form that negates the teaching of the apostles. Evangelicalism seems to have lost the fervency that gave it power for so many decades. Churches preach a message of consumerism that has little to do with the Cross. Governments have long since turned away from the Bible as a source of wisdom and absolute truth. They have no moral authority to heal bleeding cities. Individual people have little hope for a better future.

We live in a post-Christian era. Protestant Christianity birthed liberalism when it embraced social needs as partner to the call to evangelism. Liberalism died and poisoned our country when it rejected the lordship of Jesus Christ. From this near-death experience we need reviving, first the church and finally the culture.

True revival always involves the lordship of Jesus Christ over individuals and institutions. The near-dead church is revived when it surrenders its will to the Master. Revival is like renewal in that it involves personal responsibility.

Revival is a resuscitation of the church that begins with individual acts of repentance and ends with the power to transform a community. Sometimes revivals even breed whole new Christian movements or church denominations.

Awakening

An awakening is larger than a revival. American society has always benefited from revival, but often only locally and with a short-term effect. Campus revivals such as those that spontaneously touched colleges on the eastern seaboard in the 1930s are examples of this phenomenon.[2]

Four times in its brief history, the United States has awakened to God and His majesty. Major revivals include:
- The Great Awakening (1734–1743).
- The Second Great Awakening (1822–1837).
- The Missionary Awakening and Pentecostal Revival (1886–1905).

- The Charismatic Awakening/Jesus Movement (1967–1980).

Each awakening birthed a return to the Bible as God's spoken directive for guiding the affairs of men. The result was more than a return to a message of holiness in the churches and a renewed interest in church attendance. The important mark of a spiritual awakening is that the social mores of even the unconverted change to approximate those of the Christian consensus. Even non-Christians come to experience the grace and generosity of God as they observe His values and principles for living. The society literally awakens to the work of the Spirit and to the lordship of Christ.

The difference between a revival and a widespread spiritual awakening seems to lie in the readiness of the culture to turn from its wickedness. However, we fail to live up to our calling as pastors and leaders if we don't consider the possibility of our lives and strategies having a positive (or negative) impact on any expanding move of the Spirit. The infrastructures of church and community must yield to the changes wrought in a general awakening. The church cannot maintain status quo and expect a revival to run over its banks into a national spiritual awakening. We need to lift our sights and work toward an awakening. Our culture is in decay. Without a strong move of God we may lose our very freedom to worship. Revival won't suffice; we need stronger medicine.

For our society to survive as we know it, we need a general spiritual awakening. Revival in the church will keep us going a little longer, but revival must spill over the edges of our cup into the hearts and minds of the general populace. Without an awakening, the future of our country will certainly rest in the hands of the dark *prince* of this world.

Are You Ready?

The good news is that change is definitely upon us. Major news media now willingly cover Christian events and issues. This move beyond scandalmongering finally places the church back into a positive light. The new outlook now includes normalcy as Christianity is depicted as fulfilling a value-generating role in society. This change of outlook has become so mainstream that ABC Television has even hired a religion correspondent. The recent "Republican Revolution" brought *so-called* family values back to the table for political discussion. Those values represent the thinking of an earlier America when Christian consensus guided the social affairs in our society.

Secular newspapers and magazines regularly speculate about a coming religious fervor that always accompanies the birth of a new century. They expect this one to have greater impact because of the turn of the millennial clock.

John Naisbitt, a futurist, promises a revival but says it is a bet whether it is a return to Christianity or a New Age awakening that sweeps America.[3]

Religious leaders debate revival from both ends of the spectrum. Bill Bright recently wrote a book on the coming worldwide religious revival. Others produce books and radio broadcasts warning against a false revival currently sweeping the church. It is important to note that even the naysayers use the word *revival.* According to them a revival is in motion, but it is up to them to judge its merits and they have found it wanting.

All this speculation leads to an important question: "Are you ready for revival?" We crave a spiritual movement and a return to biblical values, but will we be ready to contain and preserve the fruit of revival when it comes?

A fresh move of the Spirit does not absolve Christian leaders from the ever-present task of leadership. I came into professional ministry during the revival among hippies and counter cultural people that we call the Jesus Movement. At that time, I asked a seasoned pastor why he wasn't as excited about revival as I was. He told me he had lived through several times of renewal and knew that each was only temporary. His great concern was that we excited young leaders would stand strong when the revival was over. He went on to instruct me about the need to prepare for the waning days of revival and the business of operating church when business would become business as usual.

His thoughts may seem a little out of place here, but as we plunge into revival it would be wise to remember that the church will outlive us and our experiences. It behooves us to prepare for the long term at the very moment we most enjoy the present.

Renewals, revivals and awakenings only occur in the lives of people willing to admit the need for them. This would include a personal admission of sin and the need for repentance on our part as leaders. It further charges us to acknowledge that our traditions and our strategies may have fallen short of the need of the world around us. Our churches may be "busting at the seams" but the fields are still white unto harvest.

As we are swept over with a wave of imminent revival we must look outside our frame of reference. We must search out the best implements for retaining the inevitable harvest born of revival. The farmer must not only plant and reap, but prepare storage space, and plan for the market. We must strategize the barns and flocks of the church well in advance or the harvest will lay waste in the fields.

2

A Generational Imperative

We often think of the Puritans as tight-lipped old people dressed in black clothing. In fact, they were a generation of well-educated student radicals who left home in fear of their lives for the crime of attempting to *purify* or reform the Church of England. Most were in their 20s. Leaders were a decade or two older when they embarked for North America. They sought more than simply religious haven. It was their hope to build a "New Jerusalem" in covenant relationship with God.

Failed Parents

The Puritans prospered materially because of their godly behavior but failed as parents and progenitors of the society they envisioned. The New Jerusalem never came about because these idealistic people somehow neglected to raise their children in their own stature, let alone that of Jesus

Christ. They were so caught up in their own cause that their children were left to rear themselves on their own devices.

An Unlettered Offspring

With many Cambridge and Oxford graduates among them, the Puritans constituted a population far better educated than the whole of English society. One in 40 adults had a university degree, an unheard of ratio in their day. The new world would not see such a well-educated cohort for nearly 300 years.[4] Yet their children (the Cavalier generation) were so poorly educated that they represented the greatest single-generational decline in education in American history.[5]

The Puritans failed to pass on their abilities even through such rudimentary means as home schooling. They simply turned their backs on the educational needs of their offspring.

The lack of educational foresight is understandable in a frontier situation where trapping and shooting might seem more important than reading and writing. Had that been the only shortfall, history would offer a shinier picture of this first generational baton-passing in American history. However, the clouds were darker on other fronts.

A Violent Lifestyle

"'A wicked and perverse generation,' the young Quaker Josiah Cale called his peers as he toured the American colonies at midcentury . . . a peer group of pluck, materialism, and self-doubt."[6] The Cavaliers lived in opposition to the values of their elders in many ways. They were beset by religious skepticism, witchcraft, selfish egotism, and routine violence. Many became pirates, smugglers and traitors. However, this was the generation whose independence toward moral authority and tradition sowed the seeds of individual freedom and free expression of ideas later reflected in the American Revolution.

Lack of Spiritual Fervor

Arriving in December 1630 (10 years and one month after the separatist Pilgrims), the reformist Puritans set up their City on a Hill hoping to build a new colony on biblical principles. By midcentury they began to complain of spiritual malaise in their sons and daughters.

"Midlife New Englanders spoke routinely of a 'corrupt and degenerate rising generation' . . . Unimpressed by these 'heathenish' and 'hardhearted' 20-year-olds, Puritans accused them of 'cruelty' and 'covetousness,' of living by external considerations only, by a kind of outward force without any spiritual life or vigor or delight in them.'"[7]

The younger generation did not accept the lordship of Christ as had their parents. Prosperity numbed the hearts of the Puritans and their children grew up increasingly aware of lives lived at variance with the teaching of the church and family altar. Frontier materialism rooted itself in biblical phrases, but without spiritual impetus, produced a prosperity that only brought a false security. Two generations later, New England pastor Cotton Mather wrote, "Religion begat prosperity, and the daughter devoured the mother."[8]

As the parents eased up on the covenant, they soon had to deal with nonbelieving sons and daughters who wanted to baptize their children into church membership. Leaders devised a slippery-slope contraption called the "Half-way Covenant" for *half-way* Christians. This allowed nonbelieving parents to participate in every aspect of church life except communion and provided for the baptism of their children.[9]

The necessary result was further dilution of the Living Water.

Opportunity and Needs

If we had only the example of our forefathers, today would be a time for despair. We face a very similar set of circumstances as we spotlight the generational differences facing us at the dawn of the 21st century.

The Baby Boom generation experienced revival in its youth but failed to pass the zeal and Christian values on to their children. We need another touch from God. The experience of the Puritans still offers a lesson for us.

The last of the Puritans departed for glory nearly 40 years before the "Great Awakening" ushered in the needed spiritual vitality that would carry the colonies through war into nationhood. No Puritan lived to see the revival he spent his latter days praying about. Things may be different for us. Though we Boomers experienced a small wave of revival, we so frightened our elders that we are just coming into the stature which past generations enjoyed in their late 20s and early 30s. This is true politically as well as spiritually.

This aforementioned "delayed empowerment" actually allows us time for another wave of revival. We can now implement the lessons of our youth from positions of influence. This would allow us to deal with the unfinished business of culture-bending repentance and the spiritual awakening that accompanies it. Coupling the crisis in morals with the fiscal problems facing our country, we are ripe for spiritual revolution. There are a wide variety of options being considered by our leaders. Fires of revival flicker in the surging men's movement. Some see hope in the "Toronto Blessing," and others find great comfort in the "Baby Boom return to church."

The current God-interest abounding in the secular media and in popular music contributes to a sense of expectancy as the nation once again searches for lasting values. Our particular day in history contributes to the pre-revival atmosphere as we tear sheets off our calendars in anticipation of the third millennium.

Generation Gap(s)

The challenge remains for us (who grew up hollering about a *generation gap*) to cross the current generational barrier and begin mentoring leaders from Generation X to carry us beyond the next quarter century.

Generation X, Baby Busters, Slackers, 13th Generation, No-name Generation—no handle completely fits those people born in America between 1964 and 1981.

They comprise the 13th generation to know America as America and the 17th generation born since the Puritans set out to build a New Jerusalem on these shores. New Jerusalem is a dream they don't recognize, either from history or Scripture. Their lack of spiritual awareness stands as an indictment against the prior generation.

We Christian Baby Boomers talk and write of revival, but ours is a mono-generational approach. The Boomers' return to church promises more growth and bigger budgets, but does little to satisfy the scriptural injunction to "perpetuate your memory through all generations . . ."[10] We long for the taste of revival we knew in our youth, but we have failed to pass on the longing. Our churches are tailored to our own needs and we often fail to think of the real future—our children and grandchildren.

Baby Boomers' Attitude

A Baby Boomer I know compiled this humorous medley of Scripture to describe his generation's view toward themselves and the generation that follows:

The Baby Boom in God's Eyes:

"But ye are a chosen generation, a royal priesthood, an holy nation, a peculiar people; that ye should show forth the praises of him who hath called you out of darkness into his marvelous light."[11]

The Xers Get Worse Treatment:

"There is a *generation* that curseth their father, and doth not bless their mother. There is a *generation* that are pure in their own eyes, and yet is not washed from their filthiness . . . There is a *generation,* whose teeth are as swords, and their jaw teeth as knives, to devour the poor from off the earth, and the needy from among men."[12] "Then goeth he, and taketh with himself seven other spirits more wicked than himself, and they enter in and dwell there: and the last state of that man is worse than the first. Even so shall it be also unto this *wicked generation.*"[13] "That is why I was angry with that *generation,* and I said, 'Their hearts are always going astray, and they have not known my ways.' So I declared an oath in my anger, They shall never enter my rest.[14] . . . the LORD has rejected and abandoned this *generation* that is under his wrath.[15] With many other words he warned them; and he pleaded with them, 'Save yourselves from this *corrupt genera-tion.*'[16] [Emphasis mine.]

The Boomers' Final Analysis:

"Generations come and generations go, but the earth remains forever."[17]

Baby Busters' Attitudes

The problem with this kind of humor is that it isn't far from the truth. The Baby Boom enjoys spiritual and material prosperity without much thought for those who follow. The 13th Generation is frightfully different. Poorly educated, prone to violence and lacking self esteem, they mistrust their elders and the institutions they built. Moreover, they are not embracing the Gospel.

No Moral Absolutes

Recent studies show that only 33 percent of Generation X attend church compared to a (decade low) attendance of 42 percent of all adults.[18] Uninfluenced by biblical standards, they are more prone than any other adults to believe there are no moral absolutes governing behavior in our society.[19]

Few Born Again

Unlike Baby Boomers who may even have a relationship with God that excludes church, this generation has not found the Lord very well at all. Only 24 percent of them profess a born-again experience compared to 40 percent of Boomers.[20] The high school graduation date for the youngest graduating class of Generation X is 1999.[21] This is especially challenging since seven out of 10 Christians are converted by their 18th birthday.

They Favor Churches

A surprising glimmer of light showed up in a survey which discovered that Baby Busters show a much more favorable attitude toward churches than all other adults. Eighty-four percent scored churches as doing "very well" compared to just 69 percent of all other adults who thought the same.[22] There is a clear potential for revival among this generation.

Stemming the Tide

We Baby Boomers are comforted by the large numbers of our generational cohort currently returning to church. Our numbers are up and we feel good about our affairs and accomplishments. However, lurking beneath the statistics is a phenomenon of church shrinkage as we fail to reach the next generation in significant number. A quick look at the growing average age of our congregants brings us to sobering reality: The church is losing ground on our watch. The percentages work against the future ability of the salt to keep its savor. It is still not too late to stem the tide. If we can make effective contact with those who will soon inherit our position, we can forestall the dwindling numbers we face 20 years from now. Even revival won't turn things around unless the revival involves Baby Busters in significant number and produces leaders capable of pioneering and leading churches as they move to maturity.

The gaping reality is that we Christian Boomers have lived up to the "narcissistic" description so often attached to our generation. We were so busy evangelizing our peers that we forgot our kids.

This is not a new problem. God rescued our country through religious revival in earlier times. He was capable of overriding the culture then as He is now. He did it when despair was the word of the day. Even after the First and Second Great Awakenings, violent, ungodly and unlearned people accounted for the bulk of westward movement following the Civil War.[23] Spiritual life meant little to them and the violence in the cities as well as prairie towns in the late 1860s approached that of New York, Miami and Los Angeles today. The tide turned during the revivals of the 1880s and through the Pentecostal revival at the turn of the century.

There is hope for another turnaround. The Antichrist hasn't yet come knocking at the door. We can and probably will see God work wonders on our behalf. As He does, it behooves us to work well with all the tools and weapons available. We should grasp every accessible means to transfer what we know of God to those who follow in our footsteps. We surely must ensure that someone adequately fills our pulpits and boardrooms as the church launches itself into a new millennium.

3

Morals, Mores and More

As we awaken to the needs and opportunities that exist, we are driven to Scripture for ministry models that run across generational lines. They abound in the lives of the prophets and in the relationships between Moses and Joshua, or Elijah and Elisha. However, the best text I can find for my own dilemma is in Acts 10.

Peter was given a vision of various beasts descending from heaven in a white sheet. The message "arise, kill and eat" was clarified by the *word of the Lord* when the gentiles appeared at his doorstep. Peter was to step across an invisible line, intentionally touching another culture with the Gospel.

This word from the Lord was confirmed when they were saved and baptized in the Holy Spirit in a single stroke. Even though he had personally experienced the Great Commission, Peter was dumbfounded to learn that God cares about uncircumcised gentiles. In spite of Pentecost, he acted like the Good News was only for himself and his Judean crowd.

Crossing Generational Cultures

Now is a day for a cross-cultural approach to evangelism and church planting. Like Peter, we must bridge to another culture. This is necessary to reach an unevangelized generation, a *hidden people group* if you please. Never mind that these people live in our cities, even our homes. It makes little difference that they share the same language and idioms. Their culture is different and increasingly unreached by the Gospel. We can benefit from six things Peter did:

1. Ignore the Unclean Labels

Peter could not minister to gentiles until he stopped seeing them through racist eyes. The Lord ordered him to change his viewpoint toward His creation. We, too, must stop seeing a whole generation of Americans as unclean. Too often our views are shaped by the secular media with its penchant for violence and overstatement. Media sources have convinced us that our children are a people to fear. Perhaps worse, they reinforce the slacker image among those who need to crawl out from under the weight of undereducation and spiritual underachievement.

Our ability to reach them will come in direct proportion to our ability to stop judging and to begin caring. This is the first and most important step. It is time for us as lords and ladies of the manor to invite the chambermaids to the banquet.

2. Embracing Generation X

Peter went home with the messengers from Cornelius'

household. He embraced them on their turf.

Traveling to Generation X might be as simple as walking down the hall to your children's bedroom. However we do it, we must cross cultures and move to where this generation lives and thinks if we hope to evangelize them.

A pastor friend of mine in southern Oregon told me that during the previous year, he had only one Baby Buster married couple in his church. After spending time getting to know them and structuring ministry around their needs, he saw their number increase to 18 couples in 12 months. Recently he pulled them all together in a restaurant for a dinner hosted and paid for by the church (they even provided free baby-sitting). He told these kids that he felt he had failed their generation and he repented of it. He asked them how he could serve them better.

Their responses were very interesting: They felt *they* had failed the church but could not specify how (this fits their corporate profile of uneasiness about themselves). Their second response was even more interesting. They asked for a *40-something* couple to lead their group and serve as role models for their lives and marriages. Far from being uninterested in things of God, they were hoping for inter-generational missionaries to come over to them.

Our travels won't be over water but across the barriers of taste in music, attitudes toward time and money, and other basic values for living. A good starting place might be watching a movie of their choosing with a group of Baby Busters (maybe your own kids) and following it with a time of sharing feelings about what you saw. You might question yourself as to whether you have any meaningful contact whatsoever with this new generation. Are there any on your staff or in any peer group to which you belong? Friendship is the first step toward well-informed ministry.

Jesus said "*Go* and preach the gospel." [Emphasis mine.] I researched the word "go" in a Greek dictionary and was uncomfortable to find it still means . . . "go." We can't wait for them to come to us.

3. Preach the Word

Peter preached the Good News. It was during his preaching that the Spirit fell on the hearers.

The myth says these kids aren't interested in revelational truth. I had become convinced that this *short-attention-span* generation would be reached only by witnessing, firsthand, the power of God through prayer. I thought they would not respond to careful Bible teaching. I discovered I was wrong. They need both.

Recently, I spent an hour in a backyard talk with three Christian members of a secular punk-rock band. I found that they were pretty involved in sharing the Gospel by praying with whomever they met on a music tour. Their intended converts included gas station mechanics and owners of night clubs. Two of them had even shared their faith with university philosophy professors during classroom debates. Their attempts were well intended but fell short when confronted with intellectual challenges to Christianity. Their answer boiled down to "you just have to take it by faith." We talked through some apologetics behind a pickup truck late that night. They got so excited that they gathered a few of their friends, and we would spend every Thursday night in my living room reading C.S. Lewis and watching Francis Schaeffer (who they dubbed their *friend,* "Frank") videos.

I had failed to engage these kids and therefore hadn't fully preached the Gospel to them. Because I didn't know them personally, I did not have a full knowledge of their hunger. Now I take note of their questions to be sure that I address them in my Sunday preaching. Christian apologetics are as interesting and needful to them as they ever were to my own generation. They even become a common denominator, bonding one generation to the next as we seek to better understand the God we serve.

4. Allow God Some Elbow Room

God shocked Peter by baptizing people with the Holy Spirit before they were baptized in water. Peter wisely stood back as God did the unusual. *Unusual* seems the word of the week in North American church circles. Whatever you make of all the phenomena (laughter, falling down in ecstasy) coming out of Toronto and other places, you must admit that it has its precedent in the history of American revivals and awakenings.

During the Great Awakening, 18th century Christian people fell down with fear. They shook so hard their knees banged together. Men and women shrieked as though wounded in war and many were given to visions.[24]

The Second Great Awakening was accompanied by a wide array of fantastic spiritual manifestations and accompanying human responses in the frontier. The same awakening carried but a gentle blowing of the wind of the Spirit as it swept over Yale University and throughout New England.[25]

The mid-19th century revivals under Charles Finney and the Pentecostal movement carried much observable spiritual phenomena. In each move there was plenty that could not be explained and even the most radical leaders complained of works of the flesh competing with those of the Spirit. This potpourri of the extraordinary invoked much criticism and confusion among other Christians.

Today's history books routinely skate over those conflicts, so Peter's wisdom ultimately prevailed among the apostles and subsequent church leaders. He saw God as the giver of spiritual gifts and refrained from criticizing His unique treatment of the gentiles. Instead he baptized those converts, effectively giving the church's blessing to this often misunderstood work of the Lord.[26]

In our own circumstances, we might well remember the parable of the wheat and the tares. I personally believe that much of the visible phenomena in revival is human behavior imitating someone else's experience with the Spirit. However, I can't honestly discern any heart other than my own. The problem is that I can't really tell what is Spirit and what comes of the flesh. My own commitment is to operate with order but not quench the Spirit with criticism. Bathwater is cheap, babies are not.

5. Stick Up for Young Leaders

Peter defended his new converts to his friends.[27] When called on the carpet for hanging out with the hated gentiles, Peter stood his ground and defended his actions in light of the fruit in the lives of the new converts.

Revivals are often birthed among the young and the economically underprivileged. Pastors and leaders find themselves in the uncomfortable position of relinquishing a measure of control to people with values very unlike their own. They are called to endorse blossoming leadership and various activities that would otherwise be beneath their own sense of propriety. This was reflected in an article I recently read. The author stated that no lay-led revival ever had any real impact on history. If that statement is true (and I am not so sure it reflects anything but self-promoting vanity), then the wisest move for seasoned clergy is to get beside rising lay leadership and do everything possible to smooth their path. We could then allow the wisdom of experience to enhance the zeal and evangelism accompanying a fresh move of God.

6. Plant Churches

An exploration of the Book of Acts implies that Peter appointed leaders and established a church at Caesarea. We can assume this for three reasons. First, because he fled to this location after the angel freed him from prison.[28] Second, the precedent for generating local leadership under apostolic headship was already established in Samaria and Ethiopia. Third, there was a church in place, in Caesarea, in time for Paul to visit on the return round of his second missionary journey.[29] Church planting is of absolute necessity if the Gospel is to penetrate each new generation. Revival simply cannot be sustained if all the fruit must find its way into old wineskins. Respectfully speaking, an old wineskin may be very spiritually alive, but it is old by virtue of time and its cultural attachment to another day and generation.

If we plan to impact the future, today's local church and denominational leaders must develop thrust in the area of leadership development and rapid deployment of new congregations. New wineskins will hold new converts partly because the leaders are cut of the same generational mold.

This brings us full circle to the Puritans and Cavaliers. The Puritans failed any focused effort to pass the baton of spiritual leadership to the next generational cohort, the Cavaliers. They were caught in a mono-generational bias. We need not make the same mistake if pastors and leaders will lay down their lives and comfort to win and disciple potential leaders from a near-leaderless following generation. Like the Puritans, we cannot expect success without overt action. Passive reliance upon caught values or programs won't evangelize this generation. We must willfully reach out and touch real people with our friendship, our trust and our Gospel.

Rewards

We all endeavor to serve well. The goal is to live as faithful, fruit-bearing members of God's Kingdom. We all want to hear, "Well done good and faithful servant..." There are two verses that stick in my brain whenever I try to measure how I am doing in terms of life results. One says, "A good man leaves an inheritance for his children's children," the other reminds me to "Tell it to your children, and let your children tell it to their children, and their children to the next generation."[30]

Section II

Understanding Rising Movements

4

Mechanics of Revival

Revivals are messy business. Christian leaders forever crave and pray for them but often struggle against the very answers to their prayers. We usually envision revival as generating more of what we have. The goal is a happy spiritual experience for a lot of people. We simply aren't prepared for revival when it occurs.

The revival everyone seeks is really a spiritual revolution. Five centuries ago, during the Protestant Reformation, people died for the right to take the Gospel into their own hands and out of the control of the *clergy*. But, the suffering came at the hands of reformers as well as the Catholic establishment. The Anabaptists (precursors to modern Evangelicals) suffered greatly for their commitment to "believer's baptism."[31] We can miss the overarching work of the Spirit if we take a partisan view of those events. Viewed historically, the

Reformation was not about Protestants and Catholics, but about renewal of the European church and society.

Revival, Reformation and Revolution

The important thing for us to remember about the Reformation is that it was more than the *re-formation* of the church. It was a war that upended society. People died and upstart leaders went to prison. Martin Luther, John Calvin, the Anabaptists and a host of others brought vast change to the church and to all of Western Civilization. At one point, Luther hid for his life. Bishops marched armies in attempts to stop this upstart move of God. The Protestant Reformation was a full-blown European revolution, perhaps the most extensive and longest lasting in human history.

Renewal, revival and awakening are words that describe God's work when His church no longer effectively achieves His purposes. We must realize that all three are His way of pressing toward re-formation of the church. This re-formation was devastating in the ultimate Christian revival, the Reformation. The changes it wrought salted the earth right up through the middle of the 20th century. We may not live to see a revolution of that magnitude. But whatever answer we receive to our prayers for revival, it will share the disruptive, chaotic nature of the Reformation.

A revival is a movement of the masses back to God. It reinvokes the *lordship* of Jesus Christ over His church and His world. Old structures get torn down and new ones emerge. In the character of mass movements, it is sparked by prophets, kindled by frustration, and burns rapidly out of control. Such movements are as violent as fire in an ancient forest. They cleanse the land of choking weeds and give fresh opportunity for new life.

If you find yourself in a High Sierra landslide, the first thing you should do is get out of the way. The same advice holds for someone caught in the early surges of revival. After the dust settles you can look for any gold that was exposed in the cataclysm. Attempts to control the initial chaos can only result in either of the polar extremes of quenching the Spirit or fanning fleshly fires to keep the excitement alive. Heavy doses of trust in God go a long way toward keeping our hands off His work in the early stages of revival.

Resisting Change

Every revival will bear some resemblance to the Reformation. The dead church resists change, while new leadership is zealous for it. The very life of the church is at stake. Each party advances its agenda with little regard or respect for the other. Who wins this type of contest? Usually the existing leadership wins because they have power, money and position on their side. Those calling for change are on the outside with little ability to grasp the reins of control. This is why revivals so seldom succeed.

Paying the Piper

If you pray for revival, you are praying for sweeping and costly change. Are you willing to pay the personal price it exacts?

As a leader or follower, can you sacrifice the past for a fresh breath of the Spirit? Are you willing to offend those who offend easily? Would you sacrifice position and promotion for the sake of the Gospel? Can you embrace ridicule for clinging to Scripture rather than tradition? Can you handle unusual manifestations of human response to God and His power? Will you associate with the lowly rather than the well off? Do you have the courage to suffer the discomfort of change rather than enjoy the sweet predictability of the past? Can you trade your methods for those that might mean more to people outside of Christ?

If you can adapt to painful change, you will get to participate in revival. If not, you must watch it from the sidelines. Worse yet, you might actually make war against the very answer to your prayers.

How Revivals Start

Primary revival leadership is usually comprised of frustrated people moving from the fringe of some local church to the center of the action. More appropriately, the action usually begins somewhere on the fringe of the church where anxious people dwell. These people collect a few followers and begin seeking God. The common ingredient for fellowship occurs when the Holy Spirit meets them in some unusual way through the outpouring of His gifts. They sense the power of God and see it as a mandate to change the church.

Initial Blessing

Pastors and leaders offer their blessing to the initial work of the Spirit and may even identify it as a revival.

This message of change and, more directly, the power of the Holy Spirit quickly attract other Christians. They attend meetings outside the regular circle of the established church. As this growing handful of Christians gets more excited they begin to discuss their faith with unsaved friends. The friends, attracted to the enthusiasm, attend the meetings. They often feel uncomfortable with the language and habits of the Christians but continue in fellowship because of the love and the presence of the Holy Spirit. Some are converted and the group grows further.

New Ideas

The group invents new ways to serve the newborn Christians. Fresh lyrics and music suit the taste of the new convert. The vocabulary communicates biblical truth in simpler terms. Religious formality is nearly nonexistent. The new ways are not so much tools of evangelism but implements of nurture. There is common ground among the believers. People take the Scriptures literally and cling to them in their daily practice. There is often an accompanying presentation of God's power through miracles, spiritual gifts or worship experience.

Pride and Power

The new group bursts with enthusiasm while the mother church sees only business as usual. The revival group eventually tries to share its ideas and zeal with the established church. The newcomers often display a measure of pride mixed with an honest sense of discovery.

The established church senses the pride as well as the threat of change. Church structures and traditions seem vulnerable. Leadership moves to snuff out the candle of the emerging group. Usually it succeeds.

The new group may be forbidden meeting space. Its leaders are attacked or *reeducated*. Many converts grow bewildered and leave the fellowship. Life goes on and people continue to pray for revival.

Obstacles to Revival

Existing leadership often stands to lose much at the onset

of revival, only to gain strength if it is allowed to mature. The new, and often very young, leadership seems bent on throwing down anything that stands in its way. This assault against tradition is an early earmark of every revival in history. The existing leadership is understandably threatened by this *apparent* personal attack and throws up every imaginable obstacle.

A power struggle emerges over the way things are done. The new leadership reformulates tradition, practical theology and style of ministry. The older leadership possesses a strong interest in the past. This orientation to the past takes the form of three stumbling blocks:

I. Pride

Personal pride and dignity stand in the way of any new movement in the church. Any call for new direction assumes the old pathways were wrong. It is difficult for people to admit things didn't go well during their watch. There is the temptation to resist change rather than allow the new to show up the old. This is sin of the worst kind among leaders. It is understandable and human, but still sin. If allowed to stand, this attitude lets millions go to hell in order to sustain the dignity of a protected few.

2. Economic Realities

Economic issues loom large in that long-time professional leaders need to preserve their established means of livelihood. This is the very real need to preserve one's job. Revival threatens the positions of those who have controlled ministries for any length of time. Emerging leadership can shake up the leadership pyramid. This proffers devastation in the form of lost positions for sitting leaders. Position and self-image are one thing, the salaries associated with those positions pose a very real problem. In short, many faithful people become financially threatened by revival.

3. For Old Time's Sake

Nostalgia is the third major obstacle. People have a taste for the past and hate to give it up. I recently visited Victoria, British Columbia where I was amazed at the beauty of the old buildings and the many finely restored antique automobiles people drive. The past is interesting and lovely to view, but I prefer the excitement of modern Japan where technology and architecture are constantly upgraded.

We build safer and more comfortable homes and cars than we could have a generation ago. It would be a shame to hold up technology as is characteristic of Cuba under Castro, and the former Soviet Union. Likewise, it is a shame to hold up a move of God for the sake of human nostalgia over our own delicious past.

For any revival to succeed, these obstacles must be overcome. The new must bond with the old. The old must change as it assimilates the new.

Often the wineskins break, but sometimes they stretch and revival flourishes. The calmer, preexisting leaders who hang on for the bumpy ride are usually rewarded by guiding the revival to its more fruitful latter stages. Younger leaders may provide the spark, but still need the wisdom and perspective of older folks to nurture the movement to real fruitfulness. Both young and old must value each other and learn from each other. This requires a willingness to spend time in communication on both sides of the fence.

A revival movement that gets over the hump of human resistance takes on a life of its own. It becomes free to coast into the phase of rapid growth and numeric expansion of the church. This brings the fledgling move of God to the doorstep of every church in the land. Each congregation must then decide whether to engage or dismiss the movement. They must choose to extend love and acceptance to those saved and marked by the zeal and ideals of another ministry or to opt for the status quo. Rejection usually involves modifying theology and even distorting the history of the church just enough to justify the action taken. Those congregations opting for the past will simply watch the revival or awakening from the sidelines. Worse, they may find themselves writing critiques of the present and apologetics of the past. The choices here are crucial for both kinds of wineskins, new and old.

5

Fires of Personal Evangelism

No war ever won a beauty contest. Ghastly CNN replays of Bosnia and Somalia appear in our dreams. These are ugly pictures and something we would like to erase from our perception. World War II, the second "war to end all wars" is still fading from view. It's become a black-and-white late night TV relic of some distant past, except for one continuing memory: The bombing of Hiroshima.

Most Americans feel guilty about that event. It may have saved lives, but at a terrible cost among those it spared. To many people, the biggest war ever fought is reduced to the bombings of Pearl Harbor and Hiroshima. We have little knowledge of the four years that separate those two dramatic events.

Firepower

While Americans are largely unaware of the war waged in the Pacific, most older Japanese still recall the terror of firebombs falling all over their country. General Curtis Le May thought he could end the war by terrorizing the civilian population of Japan. Some think he planned his heroics as a pathway to the U.S. presidency.

Whatever his motives, his raids killed as many people as did the combined nuclear raids on Hiroshima and Nagasaki. His millions of small fire bombs decimated far more property than did the concentrated power of the two atomic explosions that climaxed the conflict.[32]

His napalm weapons were each the size of a small can of fruit. Coupled with the wind, they brought untold destruction to the wooden structures of every major Japanese city. Beginning in Tokyo, the wings of terror hovered over darkened communities for five months. The goal was to set as many small fires as possible. The wind would fan the flames into great orange dragons, devouring entire neighborhoods with little expense.

Those small fires raged into monsters, swallowing the economy and spirit of Japan. The cost to America was a pittance. The damage to the Japanese morale and economy was overwhelming.

Le May proved an effective, if brutal, strategist. It was an ugly historical moment, but pregnant with instruction.

The Lesson of Fire

The Second World War bequeathed a legacy of painful memories. My father and my uncles fought in that great contest. Many of their friends died. Most of my Japanese friends are missing relatives because of the war. I shudder over friends who might not exist had the bombs fallen a few kilometers from where they did.

We can learn from the events of those sad days. The lesson of these firebombs is straightforward: "A small fire blown by the wind becomes a large incendiary force." The same principle that airmailed death to Japan generated life in the New Testament. It is the major strategic lesson in the Book of Acts.

Pentecostal Fires

Early Christians set thousands of small fires all over the Roman Empire. The Holy Spirit blew those little sparks into a flame that swept over the Mediterranean and touched the far corners of humanity.

God, the Holy Spirit baptizer, lit 120 small fires on the day of Pentecost. "Suddenly a sound like the blowing of a violent wind came from heaven and filled the whole house where they were sitting."[33] The wind signifies the *pneuma* or breath of God. As He breathed His Holy Spirit upon them, He gifted and empowered those early saints for the work of ministry.

The fire was partner to the wind. "They saw what seemed to be tongues of fire that separated and came to rest on each one of them."[34] Notice that the tongues of fire *separated* and rested on each one. The Spirit would fan individual tongues of fire, rather than contain a gathered flame. The persecuted and scattered saints soon took the Gospel to nearby communities. A generation later the message dominated spiritual strongholds as far removed as Northern Europe and India.[35] Within three centuries, the wind and fire of Pentecost blew those flames to the farthest corners of the known world.

Small, Scattered Fires

The apostles did not take the Gospel to the ends of the earth; their followers did. When persecution broke out against the church at Jerusalem, "all except the apostles were scattered throughout Judea and Samaria."[36]

It was the "little people," running for their lives, who carried the Good News to Samaria and the rest of the region. Philip was a table waiter in the Jerusalem church. He became the messenger that brought "great joy" to Samaria. The apostles had to send Peter and John to complete the ministry begun by Philip and the others.[37] We must acknowledge that those were "laypeople" who first carried out the Great Commission. Every mention of a large crowd in the Book of Acts begins with one or two people sharing with just a few others. The crowds swelled as the Spirit blessed their efforts. In other instances, the numbers grew because of riotous violence against the Christians.

Never was the crowd the result of a mass advertising effort. The Holy Spirit used the words and actions of individual Christians, in fear of their lives, to turn the Roman world upside down. Far from instigating all this, the apostles followed and organized the work. Except for Peter's surprise at the house of Cornelius, this is the story throughout the first 12 chapters of Acts.

We learn more when we analyze the ministry in Antioch. The saints in Antioch were the first to *intentionally* send out missionaries. But we should pay attention to the *manner* in which the Gospel arrived in Antioch. Who were the messengers that carried the Good News to this city several hundred kilometers from Jerusalem? The founders of the church at Antioch were laypeople scattered by persecution.[38]

These unnamed Jerusalem refugees took the Gospel to Jews in Antioch while other unnamed men from Cyprus and Cyrene communicated with gentiles in that city. After their work, Paul and Barnabas arrived and took up the mission.

Until this time, the racial perspectives of the Jerusalem Christians confined the Gospel to the narrow corridors of Judaism.

The apostles get all the notice, but those unnamed Christians were really the first people to seriously give witness of Christ "in Jerusalem, and in all Judea and Samaria, and to the ends of the earth."[39]

Fire of 100,000,000 Matches

What does all this have to do with firebombs in Tokyo? The linkage is the strategy. General Le May duplicated the Holy Spirit's strategic use of fire and wind. You start thousands of small fires. A large blaze is born of the spreading flames. In other words, build *a fire of a hundred million matches.* One for each of the born-again Christians in the United States.

Modern Christian leaders don't appreciate the inexpensive effectiveness of personal evangelism. Looking back on history, they observe the huge fires that burned in the aftermath of past revivals. They then make the mistake of pooling all their resources for one big blast. This is like trying to set a forest ablaze with a flamethrower. It would be much more effective to arm many people with a single match and give each permission to use it.

Though some recent research challenges this assumption, Generation X appears to have lower materialistic hopes or expectations than Baby Boomers. Many don't believe they will ever own a home. Masters of understatement, Xers disdain Porsches and BMWs for the practicality of sport utility vehicles. They don't invade the offices of politicians and university presidents. They are more interested in enduring relationships and hunger for intimacy to replace broken families. Mass-audience Christian concerts give way to cabaret singers in coffee shops. This cohort promises less affection for large-scale attempts to further the Gospel than any generation in recent history. Their profile calls for personalizing evangelistic endeavors. Moreover, some are discovering that the long-forgotten "Socratic" method of instruction works best with this generation.[40] Jesus, as well as the ancient Greek philosopher and teacher Socrates, used this method. In this scenario, the teacher asks probing questions of the uninitiated. These questions raise other questions on the part of the learner. The teacher then guides his pupil toward conclusions of new discovery. All of this reflects committed, individual effort.

The expectations of Generation X may serve as an antidote to the weakness of modern large-scale evangelistic efforts. Large-scale evangelistic efforts require strong central leadership with lots of willing followers. While trying to marshal the efforts of individual Christians, we often limit their ability to follow the Lord's command. This approach puts the players in the stands watching the coaches play the game on the field. Individual Christians become forced spectators in a contrived crowd. Most look on while one man tries to convert people brought in the door by great expenditure of money and advertising. Compared to individuals each lighting a single small fire, this method could be christened "flamethrower evangelism." But because this approach avoids real human contact, any resulting fires burn out with almost no remaining result. A better approach would be the gathering of Christians, uplifting, equipping and encouraging them before unleashing them on their peers. Study after study indicates that 90 percent of the people in an ongoing relationship with Jesus Christ got there through the personal efforts of a friend or family member.

Constructive Arson

We must grasp the mechanics of "constructive arson." The Lord was trying to tell us something by separating those tongues of fire rather than holding them together. We should try to disperse the church rather than constantly gather it. Salt is much more useful when scattered and invisible than when gathered, neat and orderly, inside the shaker. Instead of our focus on crowds, we should spend our resources empowering individual Christians to penetrate their own society with the liberating news of Jesus Christ.

What would happen if we turned ourselves around and learned how to free each person to light a few small fires in his or her own circle of acquaintance? Cell groups, prayer meetings, and personal witness of the Cross are the match sticks of revival.

The needy world calls for a revolution in the church. That revolution must take place in the minds of leaders or it will never make it to the streets.

6

Embracing Revival

Churches devolve. Just like human bodies, they come to life, grow to maturity and enter a slow decline when new cells no longer replace old ones fast enough to maintain the bloom of youth.

A Church In Need Of Love

A couple of years ago, I visited a large church born in revival. The congregation once shed strong light in a darkened city. From the time of its birth, this church provided Living Water for a broken, degraded community. For many years, the congregation was a model for others. They were so radical that the pastor would invade bars with his young disciples and witness to the worst of sinners. His followers matured into a stalwart church and several went on to start other churches.

Stagnation

A generation later this church lies stagnate while its numbers remain strong. Babies in the nursery replace most of the old timers as they die off. Building programs keep people enthused enough to hold the attendance together. The *young people* are 40-something heads of households. They substitute loud, boisterous music for the Spirit-inspired zeal they knew just a few years ago. They imported me to help them regain their enthusiasm and begin some fresh outreach. That task was impossible because they wouldn't admit any need to change. They could not admit that they were nearing death as a congregation. The body was still breathing, and they saw that as a sign of health.

Hungry Hearts

I preached my heart out and watched about two dozen people out of a thousand respond to my words. Those two dozen were a bunch of *grunge dressers* with New Age ideas who had come to church from a neighborhood bar. They showed up disillusioned with their past and in search of a better life. There were also a couple of elderly white-haired ladies and one couple in their 40s who bought into my words. They still remembered the days when their church existed for the likes of those rowdy-looking young kids.

Outer Appearances

One young man was the obvious leader of those young people. He was saved in another ministry and carried its unique culture with him, but he loved his adopted church home. I will never forget his story of accepting Jesus and bringing his neighborhood friends into that church. His frustration was that the church people immediately jumped on him about his hairstyle and blue jeans. He had been using cocaine before the Lord came into his life. This church couldn't rejoice over his deliverance but zoomed in on his outer appearance. They ostracized him because he didn't look like the rest of the saints. In truth, they probably rejected him because he was quite zealous for spiritual gifts and quoted Scripture as a basis for every decision he made. He was an immature, but natural leader looking for a home and a nurturing environment for himself and his converts. To make my heart hurt more, I discovered that he had a call to pastor.

This happened just a few years ago, but it so reminds me of the days just before the Jesus Movement in California. We stood at the same crossroads. Our mature leadership showed wisdom and channeled our youthful, often misguided, enthusiasm into real productivity. That was not the case in the church I am discussing.

Perseverance and Loss

Those kids persevered in that church for more than two years without any real acceptance from the church. I plead with the leaders of that congregation to see how dead they had become. Once a fountain of life, they now denied Living Water to those who earnestly sought it. The elders informed me that they were quite happy with their church and it really didn't need changing. They would be most pleased if I kept my strange ideas to myself.

Six months later, those young people left that church in an ill-planned attempt to start their own congregation. They've since disbanded. As to the original congregation, they still import teachers to show them how to grow bigger and richer. I'm not sure if they use the word *revival* anymore. I hope they don't. They are not as interested in revival as they are in bloating a corpse. They want bigness instead of life. A church calling for revival is much like a drowning man. Too often, people drown because they fight off those trying to rescue them.

Death and Revival

The very word *revival* suggests death or a condition closely approximating it. Those praying for revival must confront death before they can receive new life.

We always link life and abundance with revival. In the real world, they occur in the *aftermath* of the event. I once nearly drowned in a swimming pool at a summer camp. I needed reviving because I was in such a poor state. An economy needs reviving because it is in a state of no growth or "recession." This reminds me of the economy back in the 1992 U.S. presidential election. President Bush continued insisting the near-stagnant economy was in a state of healthy, but slow growth. His opponents pointed out that it was nearly dead.

The church is like the economy. It only needs reviving if it is nearing death. We'll never experience revival at a personal level or within our congregations if we don't first admit our lack of life. Our biggest enemy here is the perception that we must keep up outward appearances. Revival starts when God's people admit to spiritual deficit and submit to the work of the Holy Spirit when it requires humility and thoughtfulness to let Him generate new life in our midst.

National Revival

A true revival happens only when the Holy Spirit can bypass well-meaning people who cry for revival while protecting the sick body from the doctor's care. Consequently, revival is sporadic and its leadership haphazard.

In the United States, concerts, seminars, Christian televangelism, and mass outreaches allow for this essential cross-polarization of believers. These events grow larger and occur more often as the revival gains momentum. It is important to note that real momentum comes from one-on-one communication between believers and nonbelievers.[41] Even in mass evangelistic crusades, more than 80 percent of those following Christ one year later are actually the product of personal evangelism and nurture.[42]

Lots Of Small Fires

A sweeping national revival only comes when the Holy Spirit can get a few small revival fires to burn simultaneously. In revival, people like the young leader ostracized by that big church are welcomed. Their fire is fanned because they send off the sparks that build fires of conversion in their peers. The Holy Spirit blows these small circles of combustion into a large wall of flame. Because these revival hot-spots are small and indigenous, they have no established network of communication. In the early days, all communion between revival centers is informal and the result of friendships. There can be no overall strategy or central hand of leadership in the initial stages of a true revival. All leadership comes from the grassroots and rises randomly. Churches of all denominational flavors join or reject an informal network of fellowship, information and shared experience. Central leadership eventually emerges in the later stages of the movement. It is usually quasidenominational, but it is at this point that new denominations are often born.

Communication Breakdown

Because communication is sporadic and lacking central authority, so doctrine and emerging tradition are not at all uniform. Sometimes the revival centers become unbalanced and there is the danger of cultist behavior. This gives the established churches cause for alarm.

Some established leaders see only the strange behavior and reject the emergent movement. They attack it in the religious media, through newsletters, and over the pulpit. Others cautiously accept the validity of the work of the Holy Spirit and quietly support the growing new movement. They embrace its leaders by giving them voice in the same kind of publications that attack from the other side. The emerging leaders are invited to give testimony at pastors conferences and youth camps. Slowly their message takes hold in the larger and older church circles.

If enough acceptance comes, the revival survives to strengthen and refresh the church and its influence on society. If the church rejects the move, the Holy Spirit must wait for another generation before He can do His work.

What Can We Do?

The seeds of revival lay scattered all about us. Tiny bands of excited Christians turn up sporadically in every community. We should first identify them for what they are and protect them as we would the embers of a fire just kindled. We should shelter them from the dampness of our own routines, fan them into flame and, above all, defend them from well-meaning deacons and elders with their fire extinguishers. If there is a message in this book, it is in this paragraph. Much of what we do points toward our best human effort. The fresh, but difficult to categorize, work of the Holy Spirit often becomes the enemy to our well-laid plans. We should take the longer view and covet what we can't possibly create while remaining more tentative toward our own plans and machinations.

Section III

Moving the Harvest Into Barns

7

Moving the Harvest Into Barns

You have to put your hand in the glove or the catchers mitt won't work. If you don't build the barns, you can't house the sheep.

Revival includes three phases: repentance on the part of the saints, evangelism of the non-Christian community, and church planting to contain the harvest. All three must occur if the movement is to awaken a culture to God's will and wisdom. If fear and misunderstanding are the enemies in the beginning, inadequate preparations for logistical needs take their place in the latter stages of revival. Logistics to the church are like a glove on a baseball player. If the glove doesn't fit, we often drop the ball.

Logistical Lessons

Logistics translate to having enough room in our sheepfolds to protect and train the newborn sheep. Some of the need is met through expansion of existing churches, but more churches and networks of churches are necessary to really get the job done.

The church in Japan is a good example of this need. Christian leaders across the country pray faithfully for a major revival. In the early 1990s many were praying that the church (comprised of less than 1 percent of the national population) would grow to include more than 10 percent of all Japanese. Most prayed for more conversions, but could not fathom the need for more churches. Real estate in Japan dictates small church buildings and the average congregation numbers fewer than 30 people, yet pastors seem offended at the idea that more churches are necessary to fulfill the Great Commission. In America and Europe, revivals have always leapt over existing church structures to bring large numbers of new shepherds to the flock. But, the revivals that left the greatest historical heritage were those that produced thousands of new congregations and spawned new denominational families.

Megachurches work well where land is cheap and leadership is of the 10-talent variety. But what about us two-talent guys, especially those who labor in the bigger cities with expensive land and widespread urban sprawl?

Let's look at several reasons for planting new churches to bring in the harvest of revival:

Making a Hard Job Easier

I remember the first year of my first pastorate. We grew from a handful of people in an abandoned church building to just over 200 attendees. Because our denomination was still small, I became something of an "expert" on growing churches. My bubble burst the day I realized my wife had more households on her Avon route than I had people to preach to each Sunday. Her door-to-door cosmetic service got me thinking, and I observed that our entire congregation was smaller than the population of the city block where our church building was located. Most depressing was the fact that we had run out of space to grow. In a Los Angeles County beach town, land was hard to come by. I realized that doubling the size of the church would be much easier if we started a second congregation.

Multiplying Resources

That original church now numbers over 2,000 members but it has grown to an estimated 20,000 by multiplying itself through more than 100 daughter and granddaughter congregations. C. Peter Wagner writes, "New churches are the best evangelistic tool under the sun."[43] If he means they make evangelism easier, I agree.

Had we not planted churches, we would have never evangelized all those people. Growth-restricting obstacles come in the form of *hardware* (land and buildings), and *software* (leadership and organizational development). On the hardware ledger, land costs are surmountable, anti-growth city councils often prove more difficult. When it comes to software, I think I have a spiritual gift of leadership development. However, I know I could have never trained and supported the leadership to reach 20,000-plus people in one location.

A Most Effective Means

New churches often evangelize, assimilate and grow at a faster rate than the congregations that mother them.

Wagner cites research which examined churches in California's Santa Clarita Valley in 1986. The finding was that older churches were baptizing four persons per 100

FRIENDS: How to Evangelize Generation X

members while the newer congregations averaged 16 baptisms per 100 members.[44] This occurs for an abundance of reasons. New churches lack tradition and are friendly to recently-saved people. Pastors of pioneer churches are usually younger men with something to prove. The pastor may work harder in order to insure financial security and a regular paycheck when the mother church support is taken away. New churches filled with new converts quickly assume momentum that existing congregations would drool over. This means the established congregation can *easily* increase its contribution to the Kingdom by investing time, money and people into new congregations.

Surveys indicate that new congregations evangelizing and baptizing at the rates put forth by Wagner (above) are more effective than many of the other efforts that call for our resources. Stadium-based *crusade* evangelism reaps about one-third of one percent of its attendants baptized and in church attendance one year after the event.[45] That would compare similarly to Campus Crusade for Christ's "Here's Life" effort. This monumental telemarketing drive netted thousands of decisions for Christ but little actual change in lifestyle. A survey one year later showed a mere one-half percent of the converts baptized and attending church. This was more personal and more successful than the stadium crusade but still doesn't compare to Wagner's church statistics.[46] Recent telemarketing efforts don't fare much better. A poll by the Barna research group shows that 62 percent of unchurched people contacted in this fashion were irritated by the call. Eleven percent said they would seriously consider attending the church, while 49 percent said the call would cause them to "make a mental note to avoid that church."[47] Christian television appeals to older people who are often already saved.[48] If all this is true we would do much better investing our resources in new churches that are forced to rely on face-to-face evangelism.

Benefits to Existing Churches

Church planting benefits the existing churches in a variety of ways:

- It stimulates vision in the mother congregation.
- Church planting makes for more churches in the community, bringing visibility to the Gospel in the same way that more restaurants give visibility to the fast food industry.
- A growing number of churches even bestows political power on the church. More Christians equate to a larger block of voters foisting godly values upon the political horizon. But there are other, subtler ways in which the existing church is benefited by pioneer efforts.

New Wineskins for New Wine

We are not called to destroy old wineskins with new wine. Revival gives birth to new ideas and different traditions. It engenders new leadership that can upset a still functioning, but set-in-its-ways church.

Jesus never criticized old wineskins for being old. In fact, He said the old wine was valuable and that men would desire it over the new. He did clearly state that old wineskins would be broken by new wine and that the Father was faced with the need to preserve both the new wine and His older wineskins. New churches make the fruit of evangelism much more palatable to those who are paying the bills brought on by revival. Techno-pop music and punk rock haircuts are as far removed from the needs of Baby Boomers as were heavy metal and VW vans from the needs of our parents during the Jesus Movement. New churches allow transgenerational evangelism with peace.

Pruning Fruitful Branches

Church planting offers another benefit to older congregations. This is understood in the principle of pruning. By sending out established leadership, a church can most easily grow and regain momentum. Removing the *terminal bud* from a branch will cause a bush or vine to multiply fruit-bearing branches. The same effect occurs in churches. Remove a primary leader from a key position (for positive reasons) and the church will necessitate replacing that seasoned person with several less-skilled leaders. Time and experience will turn those replacement leaders into fruitful multipliers of the original ministry. Just as in nature, the initial loss of form and beauty quickly turns to productiveness.

The Saturation Situation

There are never enough churches in a community until everyone in that community has been confronted consistently and effectively with the Gospel by the members of those churches.

I was recently asked why I "can't stop talking about planting new churches when we already have lots of small churches in our community."

The questioner was sincere and meant no harm. He simply wanted to know why I would constantly espouse birthing new congregations when there are so many half-empty church buildings. Of course I gave him the reasons I mentioned above when we discussed the new church as an effective tool for evangelism. There is an even greater reason to plant churches and that is the effective saturation of our communities with the Good News.

Numeric Penetration

We need one church for every 200 people to truly saturate the country, assuming 75 people per congregation as the median congregation size. That would allow room in church for the 40 percent who already say they are born again. Today, there is one church for every 900 people in the United States. I live in Honolulu which has a large Buddhist population but still manages to sport one Christian church per 1,300 persons. I recently surveyed Los Angeles by counting churches in the phone book; they are worse off than Honolulu with about one congregation for every 6,000 residents. Thousands of new churches would benefit this city that has given us so much in the way of birthing the revivals of the 20th century.

Penetration of Thinking

Los Angeles is the birthplace of the Pentecostal revival, the Charismatic Renewal and the Jesus Movement. Megachurches abound. The city is the historic kickoff site for Billy Graham's ministry. James Dobson and Chuck Swindoll began their media ministries there. The list is endless, yet Los Angeles is in trouble. The streets are among the most dangerous in the nation. The divorce rate rivals any city in the world. Large visible ministries have not accomplished what only the local neighborhood church can. Churches are needed to penetrate culture with the message and values of the New Testament. Jesus said we were to make learners of all men.[49] Making learners takes more than preaching, it requires well-organized, close-order attention to people and their needs. It demands the friendships and deep fellowship that only the church can bestow.

Cultural Penetration

Long ago I discovered that people like to be with others who are much like themselves. Our home groups started in diversity but our members found ways to get around our geographic jurisdictions in order to be with their friends. They *age graded* our ministry over our widespread pleas for a geographic orientation. While we finally awoke to the age and marital status groupings, another form of selection crept into the ministry. The surfers in our church were joining ranks in home groups. This looked exclusive until we noticed that the golfers and the quilters were acting similarly. Even the fishermen managed to find each other, swapping lies about the big ones that got away while they studied the Bible and prayed for one another.

The truth finally dawned: People grow the fastest when they worship, learn and fellowship with others who reflect their own values. This may not be so important when we limit the discussion to surfers and fishermen, but it is vital to recognize when dealing with immigrant cultures, racially-torn neighborhoods and different politically-oriented people groups. Only a rush of new churches can hope to satisfy the needs for diversion we will encounter when we meet revival.

Section IV

Shifting Our Paradigms

8

Rethinking Our Churches

Our Christian worldview is like a camera with two lenses and a filter. Trouble is, we often operate as if the filter was the whole camera.

Think of the two *givens* as the lenses. The Bible is a given. It is the unchanging, immutable word of God and ought to be the benchmark for everything we do. A second given is the culture we are called to evangelize. Ever changing and corrupted by sin, it is a given nonetheless. You have to take it as it stands because you have little or no control over it.

The final element in this illustration is a filter. In a camera the filter aids the lenses by modifying the light that passes through them. In this case, church tradition becomes the filter that modifies the light of truth as we try to pass it through the lenses of Scripture and culture. The light that is finally applied to the film of human hearts makes a photographic impression on their souls. If we employ an adequate filter, the picture turns out. Wrong filters distort and destroy photographs.

Seeing church tradition as a filter will help us to correct the language and trappings we attach to the Gospel as we present it to unchurched people. Our own history and success can be the obstacle to effective communication with a new generation or people group. Today's user-friendly churches address this issue as it applies to face-to-face contact with the unchurched.

Tradition in the Church

An even larger issue often remains unnoticed. What filters have we allowed to color our relationships within our own churches? Specifically, who defines this thing called church? The culture certainly should not define the church. We easily agree that the secular culture cannot comprehend the purpose of God for the church and would not allow it to delineate our congregation and its approach to ministry.

The most obvious specifier of church life ought to be the Scriptures. That is the answer we are most comfortable with, but it often fails to address our actual practice. Too often the old saints, who have gone before us, define our churches. Church history and tradition have an almost insidious way of dictating behavior in the average congregation.

Tradition tends to concentrate power in the hands of those who best understand the tradition. This phenomenon forces newcomers to the outside edges of the photograph or out of the range of the view finder. Tradition becomes more than a filter at this point, it usurps the authority of the photographer.

To use another illustration, the typical church operates

something like a restaurant. A couple of people cook the meal, a few others run their legs off serving it and the vast majority simply put on weight, pay the bill, and tip the help on the way out the door. Some of these spiritual restaurants are very prosperous while others give off the atmosphere of a greasy spoon. Both ends of the spectrum fall short of the church as presented in the New Testament. First-century Christianity was participation oriented, our modern traditions are not.

Called Out to Learn (and Do)

Jesus said when two or three get together in His name, He will be in our midst. He said His Spirit will teach and guide us into all truth. He said we are to make learners of all nations. He said He would build His followers into a *church* or a group of people *called out* to manage a city or the spiritual environment in that city. The Greek word for church, *ecclesia,* describes a group called out to offer spiritual government. The Japanese term for church is *kyokai.* The meaning of the *kanji,* or Chinese characters, for this word is "learning society." Though evangelized centuries after the New Testament was written, the Japanese got to the heart of the church. Biblically, a church is a place for learning the truths of God in order to offer influence upon the surrounding culture. This is why leaders in the church are commissioned to "prepare God's people for works of service . . ."[50]

A church ought to function like a football team. The coaches should instruct and inspire while the players take the field in an attempt to win games. In church we often trade places between the coaches, the players and the spectators. In our situation, the players sit in the stands while the coaches consistently lose to their *adversary* on the field. Meanwhile, the real spectators are locked outside the stadium, bored with the whole process.

Clergy and Laity

Our enemy is our own tradition. We've filtered raw-boned New Testament ministry out of our churches with our programs and our finery. A return to the concept that made every member a missionary to his own culture is in order here. Instead of entertaining the saints, we should place responsibility for ministry on their shoulders and then teach to the needs they feel as they begin to shoulder that responsibility. If we can escape the duality of thinking that deems some *clergy* and others *laity,* we will win more games. Our tradition molds most of our people into uninitiated watchers and leaves a few others in the role of exhausted servers and entertainers.

The term *layman* suggests a person not belonging to a particular profession or specialty. This would apply to rocket science or household plumbing. The layman is the unlearned. In the church sense it is one who is not a member of the clergy, therefore ignorant of the deeper things of God. *Clergy,* on the other hand, is a term to suggest expertise. The clergy are that group of men and women who are ordained as religious leaders and servants of God.

There is certain truth to this distinction as would be immediately obvious from my football illustration. The problem has little to do with knowledge or even rank. It is one of position. Players belong in the game and coaches on the sidelines. Any preparation for revival must take this into account or where will we find labor for the harvest?

A church must exist to prepare ordinary people for faithful, fruitful service to Jesus Christ on the playing fields of the world.

A Paradigm Shift

A paradigm shift is in order here. We need to rethink our traditions and change them wherever they fail to approach the biblical ideal. A word of caution would note that traditions don't all come from saints who have already left this world. Many of our traditions are of our own making or just came to us from the last pastors conference we attended. If an activity turns able-bodied and willing Christians into spectators, it is suspect. If it calls a person into ministry, it probably fits the kind of New Testament strategy that would allow for table waiters and fear-scattered saints to go start churches.

You might do an inventory of your church both in terms of schedule and budget. Where do you spend your resources? How much goes to meet *felt needs* and make people feel better about themselves or your organization? Which resources and challenges really prepare them to extend the Kingdom or even to assume oversight of a group of new converts in case of revival? Your answers are critical to the ultimate success of your own ministry and certainly to any long-term effect from revival.

I once took a class under the author and teacher Elmer Towns. In my formative years he set forth a challenge I've never forgotten. He said two measures of greatness in ministry would be to effect change in the world more than one hour away from where you live and to leave the world still changing two generations after your death. Both calls require that a man focus his ministry on making disciples rather than making converts. Both criteria call us to structure our ministry and church for coaching people toward action rather than just enriching their spiritual lives.

9

Rethinking Education

Historic turning points are easily over-looked. Henry Ford is the "father of the modern assembly line." But few remember him as the genius who sparked a revolution in family finance and created today's huge credit industry.[51] By raising wages and lowering the cost of cars, Ford gave every working man the opportunity to become a car owner. Car loans paved the way for cheap credit and long mortgages, jarring American history and culture forever.

Christopher Columbus was another history-bending visionary. His genius lay not in discovering the roundness of the planet. Many acknowledge that Columbus' claim to fame was that he broke fear and tradition by willfully sailing out of the sight of land. In a daring search for an alternate trade route to Asia, he discovered the New World. Free-thinking sailors and entrepreneurs immediately began poking for a way around, under or through it. Some spent their entire careers looking for a short cut to the Pacific. It took 200 years for people to postulate that what they found was more important than what they were looking for.

Revolutionary Moments

Ford built a bigger market and Columbus found a bigger world. They stretched the realm of possibilities in their day. Coinciding with this, the first-century Christians planted churches. They did it almost by accident and were certainly motivated by fear. Their experience differs from the 20th century where church planting often is a derivative of anger and frustration expressing themselves in a church split.

Revival movements also spawn churches, mostly by accident in the early stages. Back in the 1970s during the Charismatic Revival/Jesus Movement, many churches returned to a modified apostolic model for raising leaders and planting churches. The entrypoint into formal and professional ministry began with the act of appointing laymen to staff positions. It is important to remember that this was a revolutionary idea in the United States at the time. The inevitable happened when fast-growing churches ventured into reproduction with men they had trained in-house. Laymen, simply recruited to strengthen the pastor's hand in growing churches, discovered that they were gifted to reproduce his ministry in a nearby community. From the Calvary Chapels in Southern California to men like Bill Hybels in the Midwest, formal education gave way to rapid expansion of the church through lay-trained pastors.

It has taken two decades of expansion to realize that what we got was more important than what we were looking for.

The decision to include "laypastors" opened the door for wholesale midlife career change among mature men. It gave us access to men who had been on the planet long enough to have their house visibly in order. We found a new category of labor for the harvest. We've returned to our roots and grow accordingly. Revival changes all the equations. The key to the future will be our ability to bridge to the next generation using this powerful biblical tool.

Jesus and the Twelve

Jesus and the twelve provide the baseline model for equipping the ministry. His training of the apostles was highly relational, offered a low teacher-to-student ratio, provided immediate hands-on experience, and is easy to reproduce. It should be our *primary* method of training for ministry. But, it should not be the only model for training.

The True Mission of a Bible School

There are those who would destroy lay training as resource and recast the Bible school as the "hole in the hourglass." On the other hand, a radical itinerant evangelist I once heard suggested that he would like to blow up every Bible college and seminary in the land. Both opinions only do damage to the church. We need balance between our old methods and the new. The schools are a necessity but we cannot live without the laypastors. Is there a way these two systems can enhance each other? Before we attempt a marriage between the two, we should examine the mission and value of the Bible school.

Apples and Oranges

I recently received a call from a friend. He was involved in a headquarters discussion about licensing pastors for Foursquare churches. It seems an influential businessman in one of our churches had complained that his child was attending LIFE Bible College (at dad's expense) to get a pastor's license. A staff pastor in this man's home church held license by virtue of his responsibility. The man was frustrated that the staffer obtained the credential without expending the time or money required by this businessman and his offspring. He saw our movement as giving away "free" licenses. I was called because my two children attend the Bible school while our church is a heavy user of the lay licenses. My friend wanted my opinion as a user of those *free* licenses and a *buyer* of those won by hard work in the classroom. I reminded him about the differences between apples and oranges.

A Poor Gateway

A seminary or Bible college educates people in the Scriptures but provides limited hands-on training opportunities for ministry. It serves well when allowed to function as a gift to the church, but not when called upon to serve as a singular entrypoint into ministry. Credentials for ministry are the joint product of the Holy Spirit and the judicatory structure of the denomination or local church.

To cast the professional educational establishment as the fount of licensing authority (like the businessman above) is to build a bridge on weak pylons. The system which does so makes several key mistakes about the training process. The following seven examples illustrate these mistakes:

I. Confuses Education with the Holy Spirit

Credentialing is His role. The apostles and self-taught giants like G. Campbell Morgan are joined by everyday people who would grow up under the Spirit's guidance within the ranks of a local church. Where would we be without Bill Hybels or Greg Laurie? These men are lay-trained pastors of two of the largest churches in the United States.

2. Confuses Classroom and Ministry Skills

A diploma is earned by diligent study, good writing, and an ability to take tests. It does not ensure the compassion, leadership skill, or spiritual gifts requisite to ministry. The school can enhance a minister, it cannot create one.

3. Ignores the Law of Reproduction

All creatures reproduce in kind. When making disciples, we reproduce ourselves. This applies to professors as much as pastors. A pastor will build a value system into the life of those he mentors. A professor will do the same. The difficulty lies with the application of those values in the local church; one set fits easily while the other requires careful adaptation.

4. Overlooks Paul's Order of Evangelism

Win converts, make disciples, plant churches. Paul kept it simple and there was no hiatus for an away-from-home training school. He appointed elders within days of their conversion. They qualified for the title by virtue of the length of their tenure in the Lord compared to those they would serve. This is no plea for that kind of recklessness, but we should rethink the order of events. We can bring a convert into ministry by virtue of spiritual table waiting (think of Stephen and Philip). Faithful table waiters preached the Gospel in the early part of Acts. We can bring those who are faithful in the small things into oversight of large things and find a way to add a seminary or Bible college experience to their toolkit while they remain in service.

5. Forces Unrealistic Goals on Schools

More Bible college and seminary graduates drop out of ministry than continue after the first two years. If the schools are held responsible for populating all our pulpits, they can only fail. If seen as an adjunct to a larger system, they are an emphatic success. Fully embracing off-campus continuing education for training working laypastors would afford rampant opportunity to bless the churches.

6. Locks Out Proven Success

By virtue of age, family responsibility and personal achievement, the midlife recruit is tethered to his locale. Those characteristics which deem him a worthy candidate also tie him to a local income source. Bible school as the only gateway to a pastoral license often geographically eliminates this person from pastoral ministry because it usually demands relocating to a campus center. If seen through the experience of the burgeoning churches born in the Jesus Movement, such a loss is unthinkable.

7. Locks Out Economically Deprived

Nearly everyone recognizes the reality of homogeneity in the church. People respond to people most like themselves. We also understand redemption and lift. It becomes difficult for the long-evangelized to reach their neighbors. This difficulty occurs because the redemptive power of the Gospel raises their primary values, consequently raising their standard of living. This changes their outlook in such a way that they no longer have much in common with those they seek to evangelize. These factors make it difficult to keep the Gospel alive in very poor neighborhoods and immigrant communities. An even more sinister threat is the fact that a seminary or Bible college degree is priced out of sight for most people living in economically-distressed circumstances. If we hold to a professional education before we allow someone to minister in an inner-city area, we are effectively denying the Gospel to that community. Coupled with the fact that fewer of Generation X will make it through an educational institution, we face the danger of hobbling the Holy Spirit in His efforts to redeem our society.

A Vanguard Movement

The arguments about schooling also concern the quality of education. They are hardly new. Lyle Schaller states that "those who today complain that too much education can ruin a person for the pastoral ministry are echoing a five-hundred-year-old cry."[52] He goes on to note that specialization and increased education have not produced a measurably better product in medicine, law, education or clergy and have only succeeded in pricing many out of the market.[53]

Schaller's arguments place lay-training systems at the vanguard. He says the trend of the future is toward pastors and leaders raised up by mentoring or local church training systems and a move back to the ministry as a perceived vocation or calling, rather than a profession as it stands today.[54] Others note that current clergy training and compensation practices work in the suburbs but fail in the inner cities and in sparsely-populated rural areas.[55]

A Great Enhancer

None of these observations reduce the value of a seminary or Bible college. The more education the better. It is the *role* of the school that should be examined. Here are three irreplaceable benefits provided by formal schooling:

Stabilizer to the Parent Organization

Clothing styles may come and go on campus. But theological fads and ministry gimmicks have a hard time penetrating the thinking, teaching and writing of faithful professors. Thus, the school assumes a role as keeper of the core doctrines of any movement. This seems of little weight at first glance. A closer look will show an ever-changing society shredding its values in an avenue of instant communication. Being so technologically astute, Generation X is particularly needy in this regard. Theology is actively discussed and often distorted daily on the Internet. Because of the rapid change brought on by technology, we need the time-worn stability provided by our schools. When allowed to anchor our theology and worldview, they become a firm foundation and good balance for grassroots training within the local church.

The Rich Heritage of the Campus Experience

Years spent together in dorms and classrooms generate a network of future leaders for the denominational family. Shared experiences forge ties for the inevitable in-service leadership pyramid. Locally-trained leadership can never provide this organic infrastructure so necessary to our future. Lay-trained pastors can and will participate and hold office, but they may not possess the "network" necessary to actually build the pyramid. School years cement relationships for life and give strength to decisions regarding appointments to power positions in later life. An "old-boy network" may be out of vogue, but it still defines much of society. Such a network among church leaders is immensely valuable to our future, if it can operate under the guidance of the Spirit. Wisely-run religious networks, often born in late-night dormitory talks, will embrace the locally-trained pastor. They will refresh their corporate hearts on his often unique thinking. They will also format his ministry and embrace him in their power structures.

A Reproducible Educational Experience

The classroom-trained pastor is positioned and called to duplicate his knowledge in others. He has been given much, and much is required. The school can graduate people who see themselves as walking seminaries. As these people disseminate their knowledge to a handful of disciples, they create another round of laypastors. Every graduate can and should duplicate himself in a dozen or so people in the course of a lifetime.

The parachurch movement of the late 1940s and early 1950s addressed weakness in the existing church structure. It is no accident that the larger of them (Campus Crusade for Christ, Billy Graham Evangelistic Association, The Navigators, Young Life, and Youth for Christ) all focused on the need for discipleship and leadership development. Later parachurch groups like Youth With A Mission took the process one step further when they finally took on the task of planting churches. Meanwhile, the church got back into the act with locally-trained pastors. Seminaries and schools are a natural feeder to this process and will spur rapid deployment of churches if they equip their graduates to duplicate their education at the local church level.

Section V

Labor for
the Harvest

Church Planting in America's Revivals

Revival dissipates over time unless we plant new churches to contain and nurture the new converts. As these young Christians grow they become salt in the earth and bring long-term change to the secular society around them. You could say the Great Awakening brought the spiritual strength necessary for the American Revolution. The Second Great Awakening and the Mid-century Frontier Revival fortified us to overthrow slavery. In each case, church planting played a strong role in preserving the work of the Spirit until it saturated the culture with salt and light. The difference between a revival and an awakening lies in the ability to support the move of God with new churches to service the newborn saints.

Lessons from Acts

The Book of Acts offers six church planting models for our consideration, and each one hints at the training of its leadership:

I. The Original "Meta" Idea

The first mention of church activity in Acts chapter two suggests house-to-house meetings following a large celebration, approximated in today's *meta-church* teaching. This method, discussed in a later chapter, is my own *primary* approach to leadership development and church planting. House leaders followed up the large group teaching of the apostles in an informal setting. The preaching of the apostles and informal discussion among the disciples were the primary training tool for leaders.

2. Pragmatic Expansion

The second incidence of church planting is what I call *controlled pragmatic expansion of the church.* The saints ran for their lives in Acts 8. It was most practical to leave Jerusalem in a hurry after the death of Stephen the deacon. But everywhere they went they preached what they knew. Here, also, the primary training agency was the teaching of the apostles. The difference is that the learners had to follow through and act like pastors without much choice in the matter. If they brought people into the Kingdom, they had to shepherd them in the new locality and became pastors by default.

There was control, however. The apostles were available to bail them out if their knowledge and gifts fell short, as in the case of Philip in Samaria.

3. Spontaneous Combustion

Spontaneous combustion describes the birth of the church in Ethiopia. The eunuch had some knowledge of the Old Testament but needed the correction and instruction of Philip to know the Lord. Without further instruction he took the Gospel home and Christianized a culture. For nearly 2,000 years this culture hailed the Gospel as its cornerstone. The Holy Spirit capably overruled the ignorance of the partially-educated eunuch. He grew into an evangelist and probably exercised pastoral gifts or the church could never have penetrated the culture with such success. Form follows function.

4. Rapid Itinerant Birthing

Rapid itinerant birthing of churches followed Paul and his teams. They preached, discipled for a pitifully short time, and then organized churches around hastily-appointed leadership. The preponderance of training came afterward as is apparent through the writing of the epistles. This model suffered from confusion, gross sin and lack of sufficient time for leadership training. It made up for the bedlam with those training manuals (the epistles), extensive travel (return missionary journeys) and confrontation. Its strong suit included quick penetration of cultures, rapid-fire church planting and the enduring legacy of the written Scriptures.

5. Primary Location Discipleship

Primary location, daily discipleship (a Bible school) is mentioned just once, but with astounding effect. When Paul retreated to the school of Tyrannus with just a few disciples, he remained for two years. The result was that all who lived in Asia Minor heard the Gospel. This is the only seminary experience recorded in the New Testament. It proved very effective, raising up more than 200 congregations in the metropolitan area of Ephesus.

6. Single-Minded Mentoring

Finally, we see evidence of favoritism or *single-minded mentoring* when Paul selected Silas and Timothy over John

Mark and Barnabas. Strong *relational* communication of truth, much like the relationship of Jesus to the twelve, may seem exclusive as it rewards likemindedness and productivity in the disciple. This method provides unity and careful preservation of values as the mentor hands them off only to a trusted protegee. The strongest of the newer movements around us have incorporated this model to one degree or another.

A Flexible Approach

God is flexible and we should follow His example. Biblical models are many and varied. We should keep all of them in our toolkit. New Testament leaders were marked by four qualifiers: a calling, spiritual gifts appropriate to that calling, followers (you are not a leader without them), and ongoing input. They spent little time struggling with the finer details of technique. Baseline wisdom at this point equals that of the Nike shoe commercials: "Just do it!"

Current church planting attempts largely reflect only one of these methods, the *primary location discipleship* we call seminary or, in many cases, Bible college. Too often local churches are left completely out of the equation as schools provide the only acceptable candidates while denominational judicatories supply the cash and strategy for establishing new congregations. This limits the opportunities for church planting to the vision of the denominational official and the ability of the schools to graduate their students.

Opening ourselves to other methods would widely spread out our options. Any comprehensive look at the fields, white unto harvest, would suggest we should explore every method available to us.

It is fruitless to quibble about biblical foundations if they cannot be made to work in our day and culture. If our models are truly biblical and alive, we ought to be able to find them successfully operating in recent history.

Three Effective Alternatives

Seminary, as the threshold to pastoral ministry, is a recent innovation in the United States. Prior to the establishment of seminaries, there were three predominant training patterns for pastoral ministry: Congregational and Presbyterian churches used a system of apprenticeship following college. Methodist in-service training coupled circuit-riding apprentice preachers and lay leaders in home meetings. The circuit rider, while being discipled by a more established pastor, showed up for one sermon a month. The lay leader was the actual shepherd and ran the rest of the meetings. Finally, Baptists in the South ran their *tent-making ministries*. This was used most effectively in the South and on the frontier. [56]

After the Methodists, the Baptists offered the least formal training. They often merely chose the most gifted man in the congregation. He was licensed and ordained with or without the support of the neighboring churches. Their system allowed for rapid proliferation of churches.[57] Because Christian influence was weak on the frontier, the Baptists were best positioned to make a difference. Their rapid-fire expansion overwhelmed the surrounding unstructured and violent society. Unburdened by the educational costs and time constraints of the other movements, they also enjoyed the advantage of a pastor who reflected the culture of his parishioners.[58] The less formal the educative process, the faster the growth. Baptists would recruit a man based on giftedness and desire. No attempt at formal training was required of a church planter or pastor away from the big cities. The

Southern Baptists far outstripped the others in the number of congregations, and their membership numbers are just as impressive as their growth of congregations, having gone from 100,000 members in the year 1800 to 20,000,000 by 1960.[59]

It is important to note that Baptist churches and particularly the Southern Baptists have built some of the finest colleges and seminaries in this country. But they did not fall prey to limiting access to the ministry to those high-threshold operations. While building scholastic institutions, they strictly protect the concept of the locally-trained and lay-led mission church. In fact, many seminarians adopt and act out the mission model concurrent with their classroom experience. The processes we developed by near accident during the Jesus Movement are at the root of the success of Baptist churches in the United States.

YEAR	1750	1850	1950
Congregational	600	1,600	3,200
Methodist	0	1,200	5,800
Baptist	200	8,600	77,000

Denominational Comparison Growth (number of churches)[60]

Missionary Wisdom

Any system we adopt ought to reflect a certain universality. It should be supra-cultural and not just the product of our own local or national interests. My own denomination, the Foursquare Church has long built upon the shoulders of locally-trained pastors while building Bible schools adjacent to large founding churches. Overseas, they've used schools to generate *extension programs* for those trained in the trenches.

Missionaries use every means available to them in developing nations, but often question those very methods in a developed nation like the U.S. or Japan. In 1973, hailing its success in the missions field, my denomination opened the door for laypastors in U.S. churches. This crack in the door became a floodgate. We grew by nearly 50 percent in 20 years. Today nearly 60 percent of our pastors are people who entered professional ministry without a formal theological degree. Most continue to pursue education as an enhancer to ministry rather than as a gateway into service. Faithful and fruitful ministry in a local church is the new gateway into ministry for us.

Lessons From Japan

A look across the Pacific Ocean provides more food for thought. Japan displays evidence of an inverse relationship of the value of seminary education. The Japanese sustain the most highly-educated and professionally-paid clergy in the world while showing little in terms of results.[61] While Japanese national church growth (with a professionally-trained clergy) has been among the slowest in the world, the country shows great success wherever lay-led movements work in conjunction with Bible school trained leadership.[62] In days gone by, the only real revival this country ever had bore witness to the effectiveness of locally-trained clergy and the ensuing spontaneous multiplication of churches.[63]

Opportunity Knocks

We always want to make a good thing better, but what really is better? As we face the 21st century, what can we do to ensure optimum contribution to the Kingdom of God? How can we best do our part when it comes to the Great

Commission? Maintaining status quo while avoiding mistakes is merely neutral leadership. It won't bring on an awakening. What can we do positively? Imagine we were living five centuries ago: The agenda in Columbus' day *should* have been to forsake the Asian dream in order to take advantage of the rich opportunities of the Americas. Narrowness of thought formed such a barrier that it took another 200 years before Europeans saw the Americas as anything but an obstacle. We face similar barriers when it comes to church planting and the widespread discipleship that corresponds to it.

The New Testament church had a very low threshold into the ministry and presents a pattern that works well to this day. We tend to see the early Christians as crude and unlearned, so we overlook their strategies. We would do well to expand our thinking to include what they already discovered.

Here are five suggestions that could create a new paradigm for expansion of the church during a religious revival (or at any other moment in history). Taken individually or together, these ideas could put teeth into the revival, enhancing its power to awaken the surrounding culture to God and His directives for a prospering community.

I. Take a Lesson from the Southern Baptists

There is much for us to learn from the Southern Baptists. Their model remains one of the most flexible and widely encompassing of any today. From them we learn that we should strive to build the best institutions we can while protecting the pathway of informal training and spontaneous lifting into ministry. Do not restrict the process with requirements beyond discipleship and the confidence of local elders. Also, offer more and better training options to the pastors who have not had the benefit of formal training. Leave these as options, do not construct a new and higher threshold to ministry. If a man pastors without any more than the training of his mentor, do not disqualify him through an educational system.

2. Build In-service Training Opportunities

Local churches are the centerpiece of all ministry. They *are* the church. They are the natural mothers and new churches grow most easily when born from within. We should view our schools as providers of curriculum and leadership for in-service training. The schools could supply scaled-down curriculum and function as an accrediting agency for locally-operated in-service training. Videotaped classes coupled with a live discussion leader and proxy could extend classroom boundaries. There is some movement in this area. Master of divinity programs and even extension schools via satellite show the possibilities availing themselves. I know of one small Canadian Bible college which serves churches in the United States as well as Canada. Their videotaped curriculum serves 15 times as many people throughout the continent as they do on campus.

3. Raise Our Sights

We have incredible tools for planting and operating churches if we take advantage of local churches. They have the ability to tap the personnel resources available in seasoned Christian adults looking for mid-life career change. Grassroots support is a great way to raise cash as well as enthusiasm. Also, the local church can make available core members to form the nucleus of a new church. We should anticipate congregations in closer proximity in order to fully saturate communities with our influence. Again, local churches can best call the shots because of their intimate knowledge of their own territory. Our own congregation has a map on the office wall depicting our own church plants as well as all the McDonald's restaurants in Hawaii. Our plan was to put a church in any community large enough to support a McDonald's. We've nearly achieved that objective and are now looking to match the number and location of Mormon congregations. We assume they've done the demographics and their 190-plus churches look like better penetration than our fewer than 40 congregations in the state.

4. Target Inner-City and Cross-Cultural Opportunities

Many seasoned laymen could start a house church in their own immigrant culture or inner-city neighborhood. They will never do it if we *require* the expense and time necessary for a campus experience. Our history shows we can enlist them if we are willing to acknowledge the gifts and work of the Holy Spirit in their lives.

Our church is currently experimenting with two *mission* churches in rural areas. We send teams in on the weekend to hold meetings and disciple a bivocational pastor. The goal is to establish a house church. We hope to perfect the model so we can duplicate it in small rural neighborhoods throughout Hawaii. Our secondary goal is to move the model to gang-ridden inner-city neighborhoods.

At this point we must identify and eliminate several growth-restricting obstacles in our thinking. The educational process is not the only mental barrier to growth. We must begin to admit the value of a congregation if it meets regularly with as few as 30 people (our own charter requirement). We should not await the acquisition of property to view a congregation as *normal*. Finally, discussions limiting the credential of a bivocational pastor are absurd. A man with a secular income is saving us money, not hurting our prestige. He provides a capital base for opportunities we could not otherwise embrace.

5. Anticipate Some Breakage

There will be some failures involving lay-trained pastors. They will be held up as examples of proof of the need for formal training. However, for every example of an informally-trained failure you wouldn't have to search hard to find a parallel example among our formally-trained brethren. In fact, the dropout rate of the formally-trained pastor is much higher than that of those with in-service training. Neither system is superior and both are necessary to achieve our goals.

Additional Concerns

For in-service training to work, it must feel practical to the end user. Any system must see its students as clients and customers. We can't give them whatever we *think* they need, they will only buy what they *feel* they need. The pressing need is for laborers to participate in the harvest. Any tools that we provide this labor force must be flexible in schedule and content. They should be built around a small workgroup rather than a large classroom experience. This allows for a relational experience, provides a low teacher-to-pupil ratio, and permits the pastor of a small church to use the materials provided. Curriculum should be designed for busy people, since most users will have a full-time job, a family, meaningful ministry and little time for study. This is not to imply simplistic curriculum, but materials designed for the "hit-and-run" student working during coffee breaks and late at night.

Any new program must equip for ministry, not exclude from ministry. Under the guise of providing credentials, we too often discredit those who didn't participate in our program. Tools must be enhancers, not barriers to ministry if we would succeed at the Great Commission.

Finally, we must design curriculum to *follow after* the commencement of meaningful ministry. People already doing the ministry are hungriest to sharpen their skills. Those merely contemplating ministry should be challenged to do something before they are ever allowed to take a class.

From Laymen to Pastors

By the summer of 1985, Reginald M. Jackson was able to establish a new baseball record nearly every time he stepped up to the plate. Mr. October, the great savior of late-season baseball pennants was not afraid of failure. No one—including the great Babe Ruth—has ever come near the records Reggie set that year and for the rest of his career. He struck out 2,597 times in his major league career. By contrast, Willie Stargell, his nearest competitor, heard that third strike call only 1,936 times. Mickey Mantle left baseball with a mere 1,710 third strikes in the record books. He trails Jackson in home runs as well with a record of 536 to Jackson's 563.[64]

After penetrating the record books with "airballs" as well as home runs, Reggie said, "I just hope I stay around long enough to put that strikeout record up where they can't see it from here!" Do you realize how good you have to be for them to let you strike out that many times? Reggie ended up breaking just about every hitting record on the books and claims he couldn't have achieved the batting records without the strikeouts.

Swinging the Bat!

You've got to swing the bat or you are never going to hit the ball. If you don't swing from the heels, you'll never hit the ball over the fence. Caution reaps a lot of singles, but a good cut at the ball will eventually cause it to fly. For Reggie, the goal was home runs; for us, it is to reproduce pastors, not just converts or even good church leaders. The one represents a home run, the other a base hit. You simply can't accomplish great things without taking chances. But face it, lots of times you will swing the bat to hear only a loud *whoosh*.

Paul at the Plate

Paul, the apostle, stands out as a risk-taking developer of leaders. Observe his methods in Acts 13 through 19 and the messy stuff in his letters. He owned both the New Testament strikeout and home run records. Quick bets were his specialty as he spent precious little time with his converts before moving on. Leaving town was usually necessitated by persecution. The longest recorded stay in any one place was two years in Ephesus, less than half the time it takes to get through a Bible college in America. In most cities he remained under two weeks. Yet everywhere he went, he appointed elders and established churches.

At Pisidian Antioch, Paul was rejected and left the synagogue to minister to gentiles in Iconium. Immediately persecuted, he fled to Lystra where he was driven out of town and stoned. He moved on to Derbe where many were saved.

Paul got pounded in town after town, but seldom left without measurable results. After recovering in Derbe, he "returned to Lystra, Iconium and Antioch, strengthening the disciples and encouraging them to remain true to the faith . . . Paul and Barnabas appointed elders for them in each church and, with prayer and fasting committed them to the Lord . . ."[65]

The evidence at Philippi is much the same—public preaching, a night in jail and then appointing elders on the way out of town.

In Thessolonica, "as his custom was, Paul went into the synagogue, and on three Sabbath days he reasoned with them from the Scriptures, explaining and proving that the Christ had to suffer and rise from the dead . . . But the Jews were jealous . . . as soon as it was night, the brothers sent Paul and Silas away to Berea . . ."[66] Again, very little time in town, yet elders were appointed and a church established.

Problems

With so little time given to proving and improving leaders, it isn't any mystery that half of every one of Paul's letters is filled with instructions to leaders and corrections to doctrine as well as sinful behavior.

Because of his method, he created problems. More than simply making converts, he made disciples and appointed them as leaders of fledgling churches. He supervised by mail, from a distance. Without adequate and continued supervision he could not have succeeded. He would have only chalked up a lot of false starts. It's like baseball, you don't break records on the positive side of the ledger without setting some in the negative column. You will never score victories in any realm if you don't try. Or as hockey great

Wayne Gretzky observed, "One hundred percent of the shots you don't take never go in."

Paul and his peers had more confidence than us in the process of appointing elders as they "with prayer and fasting, committed them to the Lord in whom they had put their trust."[67] Maybe it was because they saw their own success in light of God's grace at work. For them, education played back-up to the Holy Spirit. In our generation, it plays first string.

Paul often had no time to put into leadership training as he was bound to leave town or die. It interests me that on the first missionary trip, he came back around to those cities after the fireworks and quickly appointed elders to lead the churches. The text doesn't say it, but I believe he worked with the natural leaders who had survived and had shown themselves capable in the months or weeks since he had last seen them. In any case his criteria for selection were much different than ours. He had little opportunity to observe these people, and even less time to train them. In most cases, they were babes in Christ; yet, they were elders in the sense that they had been saved longer than others in their community.

I've heard it argued that they already knew the Scriptures due to their Jewish upbringing. This sounds nice but these people were gentile godfearers who would not convert to Judaism because of its rigors. It is hard to believe they were that well educated before Paul came to town. If they were, why did he write all those letters to correct their theology?

Apostolic Examples

The apostles' tactics were flexible and based on trust in the power not only of the Gospel, but of the Holy Spirit. I want to live like that. The Bible says to "lay hands suddenly on no man . . ." That is a relative expression. An elder is a relative term. In a new church, you can trust leadership to younger men more easily than in a more established situation because the man is an elder compared to the others. I've taken chances in a new situation that I would never consider later on, and those chances have paid off handsomely. They were based on trust. Those people are now vindicated as heroes of our movement. First, there was trust that the Lord would reveal the right people through supernatural as well as natural means. Timothy was chosen on the recommendation of "the brothers at Lystra." Secondly, there was also the trust that God would work with these people much as he had with Paul and his peers.

A Recent History

The early history of my denomination reflects the thinking of Paul. Angelus Temple was the mother church. From her womb, *LIFE Bible College,* she gave birth rapidly and successfully.

The "Temple" was a great reproducer, but her daughter churches were quite often sterile. The ability to reproduce was somehow not passed on. The mother had a womb and was expected to bring all the births. The womb was weak educationally in its early days but it did the job. For a generation, the Bible College was able to produce enough pioneer pastors to grow the movement at an acceptable rate. When the college fell behind, we worked to improve it scholastically. It didn't work. A decade of strengthening standards and the arrival of accreditation did nothing to solve our problem.

A growth curve of our organization shows that while that

school was weakest academically (and provided no high threshold to ministry), the denomination grew the fastest. The only other time we have shown significant growth is when we moved away from the Bible college as our primary pastoral training tool and allowed some of the daughter churches to reproduce. The churches mostly innovated and built ministries in studies or discipleship training centers equivalent to the Bible college in its earliest years. They weren't so hot scholastically. Church history shows an inverse relationship between theological education and church planting. The more education required as an entry point to ministry, the fewer churches started.

Foursquare Churches in the United States

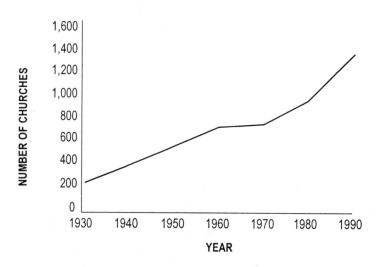

We began to grow when the daughter churches realized they had a womb and began reproducing. After a decade of flat curve, we nearly doubled the number of our churches in 20 years. Our flagship training institution graduates fewer than 100 students per year. The net gain two years after graduation is between 16 and 20 pastoral units. This isn't enough to keep up with attrition, let alone sustain the growth we've come to take for granted.

A Challenge

We must challenge, even dare our churches to reproduce pastors and stop depending upon our seminaries and colleges to do the whole job. People give birth to their own children. It would be foolish to ask the hospitals to stand as surrogate parents.

I am not trying to blow up seminaries and Bible colleges. I am saying that we better add something to the current equation if we want to sustain an awakening and evangelize an evermore distant generation. I'm not asking the guys in the denominational office to add to it, I am challenging pastors and churches to get their hands dirty and take on the Gospel. Revival is born in repentance and moves on through evangelism. In order for it to awaken a culture, it must result in church planting.

I recently spoke at a church planting summit for a denomination that strongly hails John Wesley, founder of the Methodist movement, as its primary role model. A conversation with their senior leaders was most encouraging to me. They said they had lost the impetus to plant churches according to the *Wesleyan model.* Their (quite excellent) schools and denominational offices had usurped the role of the local church. They were crying for a return to their roots and the great fruitfulness they knew in their not-too-distant past. That particular series of meetings was attended by the presidents of two other evangelical denominations. Both expressed the same sentiments. The task of rebuilding a culture is possible and the prospects look good if we will pick up the tools that have always worked the best. Somewhere in the process of leadership selection, our confidence must be in the Lord rather than our development systems. I am not suggesting that we should throw away our systems but that we should rethink them and reassess our heavy reliance upon them.

Faith

We have too many *qualifiers* worked into our programs of ministry. It is hard to imagine John saying, "Repent and go to 12 weeks of confirmation before you can be baptized for your sins." There is a healthy immediacy to the New Testament movers that we lack today. Ministry must be left in the hands of the Holy Spirit. We run sanitary operations while He brings great victory out of apparent disorder. We are unwilling to take risks while He demands faith.

We have to learn to swing at the ball. Remember, the Reggie with all the strikeouts is the same man who hit all those home runs.

12

Locally-Reproduced Leaders

Before we can fully address the reproduction of the church, we must deal with our existing structures. The questions arise: Do we have places to fit the new converts as they come? Do we have the leadership base necessary to shepherd a rapidly-growing congregation? Furthermore, can we transform the leadership base of a strong local church into a producer of pastors and elders for other churches? Finally, do we have the ability to produce the leaders necessary to shepherd and nurture a revival into an awakening?

This discussion obviously addresses physical structures and local cultural structures, but far more important are the invisible structures of love within a church. People need people. Cliques, those great enemies of churches in the 1950s volunteer themselves as our allies at this point. People need a peer group within the larger congregation to provide security and fellowship. Cliques also give rise to natural leadership. If you put any two people together one emerges a leader, the other a follower. Put three or more in a room with a simple task, step out of the way, and you immediately observe a whole leadership hierarchy without a lick of training on your part. You don't even have to offer a seminar.

We will never link repentance and evangelism to church planting if we don't acknowledge the role of the Holy Spirit in raising and gifting leadership. Recruiting and the equipping of saints are our lot. Raising and gifting are His. The onus is on us to find ways to tie our efforts to His in this crucial arena of leadership development. Cliques and peer groups are essential building blocks in this process.

A "New Thing"

In 1971, I planted the first Hope Chapel in Manhattan Beach, California. We started with a dozen people in a small building where a previous congregation disintegrated after the pastor died of a heart attack. Five years later we moved to Hermosa Beach and became the largest church in that part of Los Angeles County.

Prophecy punctuated the birth of the church. Twice in six months I heard the words, "God is going to do a new thing with this new church. It will be so different that you can't imagine it, so you can't even try to pray for it." The speakers didn't know each other and probably didn't even understand what this new thing would be. This "new thing" was the planting of daughter churches. At that time, I had never heard of a local congregation generating pastors and planting churches.

Too Many Leaders

As a new pastor, I very quickly found myself in a dilemma.

Three very distinct groups of people invaded our small congregation. Each group had its own leader. In effect there were four pastors, each with his own vision and philosophy of ministry.

I grew up in the Foursquare Church and reflect its values and traditions. The other leaders were recent converts, each with a different church tradition. One leader came from Calvary Chapel, another the Assemblies of God. The third was of the Navigator tradition. Four leaders and four different directions easily spell "havoc."

A stronger leader might have fought for control and the loudest voice. Not me. I was afraid of division, but even more afraid of confrontation. I took an underground approach. I made friends with each leader and became his personal pastor. Each would continue shepherding the people he brought. These folks were their disciples, not mine. I would look after the three leaders and my own few sheep. This way we could function as a unit with one head and one direction. Their home Bible studies became the basic unit of organization for this small church. These peer group leaders functioned quite well before joining our church. There was no need to teach them any radical new thing.

Cells by Accident

Without fully understanding it, we stumbled on a model for a reproducible church. It was a "cell-church." I was the head coach and the other men were assistants. Together, we equipped the players for ministry.

As the congregation grew, we mistakenly shed the original model. Having built lines of trust, we emerged with a single vision and purpose. At that point we stopped meeting in homes with lay leadership. We grew into a slightly unorthodox (hippie) version of a traditional American "program-based church." Most ministry took place in large public meetings with a few randomly emerging cell groups here and there. Several years went by before the need for closer fellowship forced us into the "MiniChurch" model we use today.

Multiplying Ministry

When I moved to Hawaii to plant the church I now pastor, we established three MiniChurches before we ever held our first public worship celebration. We did this for six reasons:

1. Shared Ministry

We understood the value of shared ministry in a pioneer church. Many hands, indeed, make light work. Every member of the entire body was able to involve his or her spiritual gifts, ensuring that solid ministry happened in a congregation still organizing and ironing out its wrinkles.

2. Simplified Training

We recognized the training opportunities inherent in this simple structure. Every one who had a job in the original leadership team was under orders to raise up two disciples and try to (literally, not figuratively) work themselves out of a job. People learn the quickest by helping and then doing.

3. Economic Benefits

By using lay leaders and homes we also stood to benefit economically. We had no salary structure to support and were able to benefit from the use of millions of dollars worth of expensive Hawaiian real estate at no rental cost to the church. Houses are free, rented meeting spaces are not.

4. Rapid Growth

This plan allows rapid growth. Because every "people unit" was easy to duplicate, we were able to grow the congregation almost at will.

5. Unity

We had unity. By returning to the "God authored" model of our own birth, we were really fitting into the Book of Acts and communicating a scriptural blueprint for a new congregation. The Scriptures give a pretty simple and easy-to-communicate plan for the operation of a church. By adhering to that model, we could easily generate unity among those Christians who had come from different denominational and stylistic backgrounds.

6. Early Church Planting

We were ready to plant a second church almost from the beginning. We could quickly duplicate the mother church with pastors who we found to be both faithful and fruitful. In fact, we started two other churches during the first 12 months of our existence. Both congregations are thriving nearly 13 years later.

By meeting in homes, we built a solid congregation before we paid a dime in rent. The result was a congregation of 72 well-connected, adequately-pastored persons at our first public meeting. Because no building was available, we held that first Sunday worship celebration under a tree on Oahu's Kailua Beach Park. Those home groups now number nearly 90. As a training ground, they have provided the leadership core for 31 daughter churches in Hawaii, Japan and the U.S. mainland.

It was after pioneering the church in Hawaii that we realized we have an easily-reproducible model for a pioneer church structure. Moreover, it was a wonderful tool for assimilating and developing rising leaders. These leaders work off of spiritual gifts in response to the needs around them. Their experiences pile up, educating them for greater ministry.

A Vine and Its Branches

Back to my earlier dilemma. As a young pastor I was forced to oversee flocks I really didn't lead and leaders I didn't yet fully trust. As we struggled to work out our differences, those three house churches (home Bible studies) and one weekly public meeting began to look a lot like the church found in the Book of Acts.

The early Christians met in "Solomon's portico in the temple and from house to house." We did the same and, in so doing, built a structure for a congregation of a hundred-or-so people without a great deal of wisdom or effort. The public meeting became a vine and the home groups its branches. More to the point, the senior pastor in the public meeting functioned as a vine of discipleship. The "layleaders" operated in the home groups as branches bringing nourishment to the flourishing Christians under their care.

Plentiful Meeting Space

This model requires only a borrowed or rented place for a weekly public meeting (Solomon's portico) and the homes or apartments of its members. Leaders emerge according to their gifting. The senior pastor spends a few hours each week with home group leaders. He provides a flow of communication and training. His only other major calling is the time he spends in sermon preparation and pastoring his own home group. The MiniChurch leaders and their people offer one another mutual counseling and support. This remains a low-budget operation. All leaders can hold jobs outside the church until growth demands full-time help. Surplus monies go to ministry. The model allows the church to re-penetrate urban areas where people are hard pressed for time and money. It also sets the church free from a cost-prohibitive, land-based operation. Asian churches routinely operate in this fashion.

Generating Momentum

Three home groups and a primary leader is the nucleus for a church that can quickly grow into a full-service family of Christians.

Three groups isn't absolutely necessary, but having three lends critical mass to the church. There are enough people to build rapid momentum. Momentum is important in the life of a new congregation. Operating much like a football team, the members will accomplish great things if they stay fired up. Growing numbers on the spiritual scoreboard in the categories of people coming to Christ and overall church attendance keep the morale high.

The model we are discussing also provides a diversity of spiritual gifts in the leadership core. If this works this well at a church planter's level, we can project that a large cell-group church would be in a great position to feed revival by throwing off daughter churches.

Protecting Revival Results

Revivals breed new churches. Every revival since the Reformation has resulted in some spontaneous multiplication of churches.

Historically, movements that planted the most churches sustained the greatest long-term results. The reason is simple. The more Christians you have taking responsibility for the well being of others, the more salt in the earth.

Jesus Movement Christian Coffee Houses

The Jesus Movement of the 1970s generated thousands of

Christian "coffee houses" and close to a million home Bible studies.

By New Testament standards, most of these coffee-house congregations included the basic ingredients of a church. They depended on non-ordained, but Holy Spirit anointed leadership. They enjoyed a liturgy made up of teaching, fellowship, breaking of bread, prayer, worship and a spirit and means of generosity. Most importantly, they allowed for an easily-reproducible ministry model. No salary or formal education was necessary. People were content with informality of structure and surroundings. These groups were flexible about location. Meeting places were easily obtainable and, if lost, replacements came without much effort.

As a spiritual awakening, the Jesus Movement appears weak in moral authority. At first glance, it seems but a gentle wave long since passed. But, it spawned more new churches than any previous American revival.

That short revival spawned thousands of churches, many growing from its coffee houses. Today, those churches form a strong contingent of "user-friendly" congregations. As the Baby Boom returns to church, these Jesus Movement congregations may yet spark a strong light for the world. The key lies in the spiritual life of those churches as they come of age. Churches born in the Jesus Movement are just now reaching middle-aged maturity. They will continue to do so through the first decade of the next century. A revival of holy living and the message of the Cross could still allow our generation of Christians to impact our world with God's redeeming power.

The "coffee house model" worked because it was so simple. Yet, many coffee house leaders grew into unordained "clergy" and are among today's better-known Christian leaders. The Jesus Movement should bear fruit for another two generations through these congregations.

Cappuccino Bars

Coffee shops are in vogue again. Generation X loves cappuccino bars, probably because so many live with parents and have no other place to entertain friends. Whatever the reason, the circles of people exhibited on the television show "Friends" is a perfect setup for small groups within larger churches. They also provide a format for networking the Gospel among peer groups the way missionaries do with extended families in Third World cultures. With a little luck and the willful strategy of Baby Boom leadership (who hold the purse strings), we could foster growth in this coffee shop movement. It is entirely possible that Generation X could raise a generation of new churches to match and surpass what we've known. It would be safe to say that if we don't, there won't be a general cultural awakening to the Gospel.

Primitive Tools Still Work

Jesus' instructions are still to go into all the world and make disciples of every person. He gave us the church as our basic tool. We often complicate the church and make its operations a heavy burden. The simple, even primitive models of the New Testament can work well in our modern world.

They might even work better than those we inherited from the generations before us.

Section VI

Facing Tomorrow

13

A Message to Boomers

This book is about Gen X, but it is written *for* Baby Boomers. We Baby Boomers are currently in the driver's seat of our nation and of our churches. We have the vision to project the near future. We have tremendous strategic abilities, and we have always possessed the drive to accomplish any task we set about.

Most of us will hand off our jobs to a Generation Xer. An Xer will one day stand over a hole in the ground and say nice things about how we lived our lives. How well those people do their tasks is still largely a product of how well we prepare them for their role. It's late in the generational relay race. But, we still have time to arrange a smooth handoff. Our participation is highly critical because they will inherit the earth with shrinking resources. We owe a great debt to our offspring because we've taken much from their future.

A Generation of Debtors

We borrowed from the future for most of our lives. We did it by buying so much on credit. We did it by taking time for our own interests rather than fully investing ourselves in our children. The moral condition of our country changed during our youth to meet our demand for pleasure without God's blessing. Those debts remain outstanding.

National Debt

Our government currently spends just about $15 for every $14 it collects in taxes. After 27 years of manufacturing red ink, we bequeath Generation X a debt of more than $5,000,000,000,000 (five trillion dollars).[68]

Xers express frustration at this weight on their shoulders. Andy Crouch, a Harvard University campus minister writes: "I have come to see my generation, though, as a generation of debtors—both in that we are owed debts that will never be paid *and* in that we owe debts we can never pay." He continues, "In one sense, the national debt is ours: It will fall to us to pay it, if we can. But because we were so young when it was amassed, we also sense that the national debt is owed to us—as promises made to us that will never be fulfilled. Our parents have sowed the wind, and we have reaped the whirlwind."[69]

Moral Debt

Debt encompasses more than a lack of financial assets. It was our generation that bought into the idea that moral absolutes do not exist. We held a sexual revolution. As the Woodstock Generation, we elevated drug abuse to the status of a cultural icon. We've left a legacy of broken children who are adults facing an uncertain world without a moral compass.

To whine about the national debt and the cost of paying off our mortgages only reinforces a wearying sense of guilt. We need an approach to picking up the pieces. How can we join forces with our offspring to ensure a brighter future for the church and our country?

We could start by acknowledging the current existence of a *generation gap* in our churches. I recently spoke at a church growth conference on the island of Maui. My task was to address the needs and opportunities we face with Generation X. One of the attending pastors hadn't read the promotional material completely. He kept waiting for me to get off my subject and talk about how to operate small groups. He told me this at the end of the conference. But his distaste for the subject was written all over his face as I spoke. He said it took three days to see my point. Once he shifted his viewpoint, he felt new enthusiasm rising in his heart. He told me he thought he would naturally *know* how to reach out to Xers. He bought the conference tapes just in case he missed something worthwhile during the three days of restlessness.

That pastor told me that he felt his church was "inclusive." My surfacing the needs of Generation X seemed irrelevant in light of that inclusiveness. He finally came to see that *passive inclusion,* by itself, almost always equates to tokenism. The majority group looks around to see a few of the minority in its midst and assumes they are reaching that population. Left alone, inclusion fails as a strategy for cross-cultural outreach. However, coupled with thoughtful strategy, inclusionary policies rotate into aggressive inclusion. This aggressive inclusion is the first major step in reaching across any cultural barrier. It easily prepares us for the next stage which is intentional focus on the minority culture. That leads us to church planting and Generation X.

Three Options

The first option facing successful Builder/Boomer churches is to do nothing. The prospect of a few more comfortable years of ministry centered on our needs and values is very tempting. The downside is that we face the possibility of our own children and certainly our cities living an entire lifetime outside of God's grace and influence.

The second option is much more profitable. This option is the choice to become a bicultural church able to address the needs of Gen X without compromising ministry to the existing congregation. This is certainly the option that must be chosen by most church leadership teams if the church is to remain viable in the coming millennium. Many will settle for this option and we will be much the better for their choice. We will look closely at the mechanics of cross-generational or *transition* churches in another chapter.

The final option is the most costly, as well as the most productive. It requires moving from Builder/Boomer success into a transition mode, followed by aggressive church planting. The daughter churches will target Gen X the way our existing churches targeted Baby Boomers. This will require that we Boomers reprogram our thinking toward ministry that is specifically designed toward the needs, strengths and foibles of a generation that isn't about to drive *their father's Oldsmobile*. Not everyone will opt for this third choice as it can be painful. Those who do will position their disciples to do something we cannot: That is, to fully address a generation on its own terms through leadership drawn from within its own culture. The key to effective evangelism is homogeneous church planting.

Homogeneous Evangelism

Planting a generation of new churches is exactly what our Builder forebears embraced as we came through later adolescence into adulthood. It paid the wonderful returns that we enjoy today. We know that the most effective way to evangelize any people group is through homogeneous church planting. We also recognize that churches require leaders and that the most effective leaders come from within the target population.

In my own church, we have turned a corner with the leadership structure. Currently, five out of nine members of the primary governing body of our largely Boomer church are Gen Xers. The *core* staff members are all Boomers or Builders. However, when measured in total numbers, Gen X makes up more than 60 percent of the staff. We are aggressively embracing a strategy to raise seasoned leadership for the next round of church planting. That leadership will be made up almost exclusively of Xers.

Our goals are threefold: (1) To understand Gen X; (2) To mentor effective leaders among them; and (3) To hand off leadership of our congregation, including the responsibility to plant new churches. We have become a transition church. I am operating with the primary motive of planting new churches from within Generation X. I am also very aware that I must begin thinking in terms of succession which requires that our congregation has an adequate leadership base to replace us Boomers as we face retirement.

We will look at Xers as potential leaders for the rest of this chapter. Because we do look across a communication gap, we often misunderstand each other. My goal is to show that they are adequate to the task before them.

A Generation of Entrepreneurs

Though the media typify Xers as slackers and while they may delight in dressing grungy, this generation shows a surprising entrepreneurial bent. It may be due to the economic circumstances into which they were born. Most came into a world of technology, nice houses, two cars and working parents. Those who had only one parent lacked material wealth but were exposed to it at school through the possessions of their peers. As they matured, it became apparent that much of what they took for granted would not be readily available in adult life. That realization fueled two paradoxical inclinations. Their first priority is relationships over material wealth. Their second priority is to adapt in whatever ways necessary to scratch out a living in support of those relationships. This confluence of values results in a surprising number of business startups. Church planting ought to be easy for a generation accustomed to getting by with inadequate resources while they strive to build something stable and productive.

Fewer Resources

Economic hardship is the primary force behind business startups in the United States. Gen X has less money available than any generational cohort living today. Twenty-two percent of Americans with jobs are part-time or temporary workers and the number of bus drivers with college degrees has doubled in the past decade.[70]

Xers have lower expectations than we had. Recent studies show 75 percent of Xers believing they will be economically worse off than their parents.[71] Massachusetts Institute of Technology economist Lester Thurow bluntly sums up the near horizon for Gen X, "In Europe you get unemployment insurance; in the U.S. you get a low-wage, dead-end, part-time job."[72]

In spite of the bad news and media labels, these people are not slackers. Though many dropped out of high school and remain functionally illiterate, at 66 percent their overall college enrollment rate is the highest in U.S. history. They work an average of 3.6 percent more hours per week than the rest of the workforce and nationally, tally up 70 percent of all new business startups.[73] A Marquette University study estimates that nearly 10 percent of Xers are actively working on starting a business. That number leaves their generation producing entrepreneurs at about three times the rate of any generation alive today.[74] An entrepreneurial spirit is an obvious necessity for church planters.

Paradoxically, while these Xers may have fewer overall resources, they have surplus cash at their disposal. Their median per capita income is 13.6 percent lower than it was for Boomers at the same period in their history.[75] Lower income and desire for relationship translates into living with parents at reduced rent and fewer expectations of owning a home. The same cohort who are so positive about starting businesses are the most negative when polled about the prospects of home ownership.[76] This leaves the "down payment money" available for evenings out, books, music CDs and investment in ministry.

Save the Planet

Investment in ministry *is* a priority for Xers. However, they have a different take on what qualifies for their donation dollars.

Projects are no small issue to this generation. They are idealists after a different fashion than their parents. Not bent on self-improvement, they are enthralled with the betterment of the planet. Just watch a few hours of MTV and you will discover an inherent desire to make the world a better place for anyone they perceive to be downtrodden. This bodes poorly for the church which has shunned the issues of racism, AIDS, poverty, and political suppression.

The money is available if the project fits the priority profile. The future is ripe for startup churches that own big dreams when it comes to bettering the community. Xers currently give less to churches than any previous generation at their age. The lack of financial commitment will turn around once the churches receiving their gifts get on track with the projects that touch their hearts. They will not invest in fancy architecture or slick programs. Their churches will look like the coffee shops they so willingly finance. Churches will have to show concern for more than political change or world evangelism to get their attention. Those led by Xers will be in the best position to do this and there appears to be no shortage of raw material when it comes to finding potential leadership. The ball is simply in our court: It is up to us to invest the ministry currency of today into a viable future by rethinking the way we perceive the future. That future will be anything but a gradual extension of what we've already known.

Reallocating Resources

The generation gap of yesterday produced *up-to-the-minute* churches that broke tradition and left the Gospel in contemporary clothes. Many of us would be shocked to discover that *contemporary* is an old-fashioned word, reeking with tradition, to most Xers. I recently talked to the pastor of the "contemporary worship service" at a mainline denominational church. He told a frighteningly archaic story of a board that took five weeks to approve the use of guitars in his liturgy. They only approved this musical *update* after requiring him to move the meeting out of the sanctuary and into an ancillary auditorium. We must do better than that if we expect to keep up with the Psalmist in his desire to invest "hidden lessons from our past" in the next generation.[77] We must start with the reallocation of key resources to prepare for the rise of Generation X.

Leadership

New generation churches will require the transfer of knowledge to a new leadership base. To a generation skeptical of institutionalism, this requires that current leaders mentor potential pastors for service in *another* location. Mentoring is a rewarding business when you face the prospect of a long and endearing relationship with your disciple. It can also be painful when you know it is meant to be temporary and will ultimately result in separation and loss. One of my best friends is a man I mentored for 10 years. Today he is a successful pastor and we continue the friendship at a distance. My children are active in church ministry 2,500 miles from home. Proud as I might be, I cannot avoid the pain of separation in either circumstance. Parenting is more painful than mentoring, but we continue with both for reasons that are much the same.

Money

By now, you've noticed that money is hard to come by. It is as precious to ministries as to individuals, perhaps more so. Most of our churches are up to their ears in vision that could easily blot up every dime we could ever raise. We have plans for the financial resources available to us. The thought that we may not be able to do as good a job of evangelism as some grunge-dressing young person with suspicious manners hardly appeals to Baby Boomers. Truth be told, we built most of what we have by mortgaging their future. That is probably the reason they tend to the grunge look in the first place. We should start thinking about the budget requirements we will face if we start adding young staff and the ultimate cost of sending faithful givers out the door with large sums of money to start new churches.

I spent this morning with a couple of church planting officials from one of the oldest denominations in America. The movement is old enough to have forgotten the priority of church planting. These men are trying to rekindle the fires of history. With them were a 65-year-old senior pastor and his 26-year-old son. The father and son introduced me as a consultant to the officials regarding their plans for planting churches in Hawaii. The wisdom of the father (a Builder), coupled with the zeal of the Xer son were quickly joined by the financial resources of the denomination through the vision of the Boomer officials. They offered support money *outside* their usual channels for any attempted church plants stemming from this successful congregation. The pastor and his son replied that they were willing to do it on their own, but would gladly accept the monies. Both local church and denomination demonstrated a spirit of generous investment. Those people are a perfect example of the type of investment necessary to produce fruitful churches as we enter the third millennium.

People and Relationships

The transfer of people and relationships spreads the pain of church planting like no other element in the process. We lose familiarity and even a portion of our hearts whenever we launch a new church plant. I always look forward to the birth of a new church with the same joy I felt when I became a father. However, these births also include a kind of post-partum pain, the loss of precious time with people I love. One extended family from our church recently left us to help a friend of mine start a very successful church in Honolulu. They are more involved in ministry than ever and having a world of fun in the process. It also cost them dearly. They left a daughter, son-in-law and beautiful granddaughter with us. These people know something of the cost of discipleship. Folks like these are great examples to others who drag their heels over the disruption caused by planting new ministry.

Momentum

For churches, the most difficult resource to recover is momentum. It is the easiest to let go because it is so intangible. It costs us the least in terms of emotional currency in the short run. Yet, perhaps it is the costliest resource we have when it comes to church planting. It is the only one that I spend with caution.

Every time we launch a new church, we face a period of reduced enthusiasm due to rooms not so full of people. Our worship experience is a little dull without familiar faces in the band and the experience they brought to the worship team. Our staff needs time to reconfigure enthusiasm and morale with a less-familiar face at one end of the table. The congregation *feels* a loss of momentum brought about by the investment we just made. My own job is more difficult for an extended period as I am called on to work with rookies in various leadership capacities. While there is a price for loss of momentum, it can be regained in a healthy pride over the welfare of the new church. But make no mistake: It costs you something. However, it is not an insufferable loss. Three times in my own pastoral history we've sent out 20-plus percent of our church as the initial team for a new congregation. The first time, that percentage involved only 25 people. The last time it represented 330 individuals. Each time we not only recovered but found out that pruning really does cause a branch to bear more fruit.[78]

The need to reallocate resources is not just an issue for church planters. For our own sake we must be willing to invest in them if we expect to relax under their care and quality of leadership 30 years from now.

Footnotes for Thought

In the next chapter, we will look at Gen X a little more thoroughly. The goal is to understand their very high value orientation toward *authenticity*. Being so oriented toward relationships, loyalty and authenticity leaves them expert at the softer issues of life and ministry. My own generation is known for some of the harder issues of life. We grew up very idealistic. We proved we could make the turn from long hair and bare feet into BMWs and upscale housing. We are very capable of turning our idealism into workable reality due to our strategic bent. Whatever we did, we set out to do it better than it was ever done before. Often, we accomplished our goal. If you will pardon a metaphor that sounds dangerously corny, our idealism and strategy could provide the hardware platform to operate the software of their proclivity toward authentic relationship. With this combination, we might be able to affect the next 10 years in a greater way than Microsoft affected it in the past 20.

14

■ Authenticity

Can you remember way back when it was "groovy" to describe someone else's values or likes as his "bag?" If so, you probably have a different take on basic values than does Generation X. This qualifies you to participate in the current generation gap.

Our generation either fought absolute truth or embraced it. Both extremes birthed a kind of freedom in us. We either found freedom from all restriction (the bondage took a little time to become apparent) or we found true freedom in the Bible. As Christians we were free because we held a matrix of information that allowed us to filter our world view. Our filters provided a framework for decisions and engendered personal security.

The larger number of our generational cohort rejected absolute truth and the values that sprung from it. Gen X inherited this overall lack of moral absolutes and suffers from the resultant insecurity. Without absolutes they are left with no frame of reference. Without a backdrop of truth to measure the worth of competing ideas, even common sense died. The ensuing search for authenticity is a cry for a foundation on which to build lives and households. Left with little more than personal instinct, they are looking for whatever rings true.

False Promises

Perhaps the key to understanding Generation X is to perceive their disillusionment with the world around them. For most Xers, the world is a set of false promises. This began with the promises mom and dad made to spend time with them. It continues through the implied promise that their family would remain together for life. They were burned by television promises about toys that satisfy and by the promise of safety on the streets. They crave authenticity in a world without illusion. To them, lowered expectations equal reality. They demand that reality of the world or they refuse to interact with it. To understand this need for authenticity is to open the door to ministry.

Authenticity: The Core Value

A humorous example of the search for authenticity involves the popularity of singer Tony Bennett. Long after leaving his heart in San Francisco, the crooner achieved a new popularity on MTV. Alarmed at first, he thought Xers were making fun of him. Calmed to the attention, Bennett now plays the role of a grandfather everyone can trust. In a world without standards, people have found a friendly authority figure who promises little but never lets you down.

Bennett, with his easy-going manners, exhibits the fact

that Xers have little use for hype. One Xer pastor interviewed by *NEXT* magazine put it this way: "The foundation
for ministry to and with Generation X is authenticity. Xers
have little use for hype . . . Be authentic. If I have a real
relationship with Jesus Christ it means I can admit that I am
struggling. It means I can be transparent. It means I can be
vulnerable with people."[79]

With authenticity as a measure, a lot that we do in
Christian churches looks like cheap television. "When you
coordinate the color of your shirts to the color of your lights,
people don't see that as authentic," says Chris Seay.[80] Seay is
pastor of University Baptist Church in Waco, Texas, perhaps
the nation's largest congregation pastored by an Xer. Seay
identifies authenticity as a major issue to Xers seeking openness and honesty in the name of God. A slick presentation of
the Gospel may work for Boomers but it looks like subter-
fuge to Xers. They want to clearly distinguish between
honest leaders and hypocrites.

The latest commercials and magazine ads reflect this
change in thinking. Less is better than more. Real is better
than hype. Slightly tired looks like reality and they don't like
answers that fit the question too well. Gen X runs away from
overblown promotion and shrinks back from a hard sell.
They want to be respected for having enough intelligence to
make a thoughtful decision.[81]

What Really Matters?

This generation defines success in terms that sound more
like those of their grandparents than their parents. Family
issues are of supreme importance to a group that deems
human relationships supreme. Xers marry at a later age than
did their parents. The reasons encompass more than their

financial plight. The young people in my church are bent on success in their homes. They would rather wait longer in hope of raising the odds of sparing their children a divorce.

A Christian advertising magazine came up with surprising answers to a question asking for a Generation X definition of personal success. Thirty percent of Xers identified success as a balance between work and home, while 26 percent called for a happy home life. A scant 12 percent held academic or professional achievement as the standard. Twelve percent identified spiritual fulfillment as the goal and only 11 percent saw a lot of money as the definer of success. Conversely, money checked in as the biggest stress factor in most lives at a 30 percent respondent rate. It was followed by job pressures at 19 percent. Time pressures rated 11 percent. Love life came in at 10 percent and family life was last on the list accounting for pressure in only 9 percent of the lives queried.[82] These answers clearly reflect neither the yuppie values of our recent youth or the idealistic but hippie notions of our earlier days. This generation is trying desperately to fit into the world of generations past.

God, Not Church

The rash of interest in angels and things spiritual points to a renewed interest in God. The very existence of God, the meaning of life on earth, forgiveness and even our place in the cosmos occupies a good deal of their conversation.

While God may be important, churches and doctrinal statements are not. Because this is a generation with no fundamental belief in absolutes, too many of our practices put them off. They want an experience-oriented faith and are slow to embrace a firm position on doctrinal issues. There are one-third fewer converts among them than among Boomers at the same period in their history. Even so, it is quite easy to talk to them about the Gospel. They simply take longer to believe it. For this reason, evangelism becomes a more friendship-oriented process and involves less preaching. Because they don't respect the imposition of ideas or rules, they reject churches suspected of hard-lining or manipulating.

Outwardly, they respond to a more relaxed setting where the focus is on the spiritual event. In our own meetings, they favor worship over everything else. Surveys reveal that they like rock music with an "edge" as opposed to the smoother style favored by Boomers. Ancient hymns played with a stronger beat often appeal to them because the message is more direct. Teaching without a pulpit appeals because it appears more like conversation. Suits are out, jeans or Dockers and open shirts are in for Boomers who address them. Grunge dress is definitely restricted to Xers. A Boomer in ragged plaids and Levi's is a "definite *wanna-be.*"

Forgiveness

Xers have much to forgive. This is the most neglected, abused, sexually-assaulted group on the American scene. They struggle with moral debt more than with the financial sins of their parents. Besides forgiveness toward parents, these people must cope with frightening violence among their peers. The inner cities taste a daily ration of gang warfare alongside the swell of drugs and rape. Suburban women report violence from boyfriends as often as their sisters in the cities . In our church, we often counsel young women who want to forgive an abusive former boyfriend or husband *before* they are fully willing to accept Jesus' forgiveness of their own sins. They sense forgiveness as a way to freedom. For such a generation, the Cross takes on new meaning and power. One Gen X leader in my church suggested that his peers may eventually take up the Cross of

Jesus Christ as the ultimate symbol of their generation. He said the mixture of sin-induced pain and forgiveness of Jesus on the Cross appeals to his friends like no other presentation of the Gospel.

Love

The Beatles are back and again remind us that "money can't buy me love." The children with the largest discretionary income in history sadly grew up without much adult attention. Well entertained, they lacked intimacy with their parents. They compensate with well-grounded friendships and serial courtships. Fearful of a failed marriage, they opt for a series of "going out" relationships. Sexually active, these could be termed "serial monogamy."[83] We *went steady* as a prelude to marriage. They do it as a fearful substitute.

The Baby Boom introduced hit and run sexuality. For today's young adults, sex is an attempt at holding onto someone. This amounts to love addiction. Violence arises when fear of losing the security of a lover invades the mix. One young woman in our church told us that her ex-boyfriend would punch her, pull her hair and even slammed her head in a car door. He said he did it because she wouldn't act right. Every occasion was at a time when she stood up to him or attempted to leave him. People who met him describe a polite, soft-spoken, responsible individual. To her he was a monster. Real love will always escape this man short of a trip to the Cross. To understand him is to gain great insight into his generation.

Strong and Dependable Family Life

Today, I watched a 30-year-old man weep over his friendship with his dad. He sustains the relationship with regular phone calls and occasional lunch dates. His dad is beginning to respond to the love. There is clearly something wrong with that scenario, but it really happened. Children weren't designed to initiate family relationships. The upside is that we find many Xers evangelizing the parents who never spent much time with them in childhood or adult life. The adult child having found the Lord forgives then reaches out to the parent with the Gospel. This is one of the many positive benefits of Generation X and its high value on family relationships.

Parents aside, Generation X is bent on stable marriages and responsible parenthood. A recent survey of college freshmen reported that 70 percent believe a strong and sustainable family life is essential to their happiness.[84] We routinely organize home Bible studies around a video series teaching excellence in parenting. Many young couples desire the fellowship of a home group but postpone it due to a busy schedule. Childbirth renders them busier than ever. But something changes. They suddenly find time for the home group if it promises to enhance parenting skills. Our developing ministries focus on the family needs of this generation. Their requirements stretch from anger management to personal finance. They crave help evangelizing parents and raising children. The high priority on family provides a wonderful opening for growth in Bible knowledge and stable Christian relationships.

Personal Responsibility

The days of government to the rescue are over. Encountering a national belt tightening, we enjoin it with a rising generation rooted in personal responsibility. The one theme I hear over and over from my own children and the Xers on my staff is "you gotta look out for yourself." They sure don't expect the government to come through for them. A Generation X political advocacy group contends that a higher percentage of this generation believe in UFOs than believe they will ever reap the retirement benefits of Social Security.[85]

Their immense respect for personal freedom fits this profile. They prize control of their time far more than they value money. This control of time spreads into responsibility over lifestyle. If success comes their way they embrace it, but they will not surrender their identity to achieve it. This is another take on authenticity. They look for that "ring of truth" in their selves and their presentation to the world. My sad experience has been that of losing three different young leaders who felt called into ministry. They had difficulties perceiving themselves as team players. The required compromises were too great to fit into their personal *ideal*. Each wanted more control of his or her own destiny. The odd thing (to a Boomer) is that they left the position and team, but remain in close friendship with those they rejected as partners. Without bitterness or anger, they remain in full and loyal friendship with the rest of us. They see their choices as their own responsibility and do not perceive themselves as victims of the system they left behind.

Community Responsibility

At a community level, Generation X believes the individual can make a difference. Our Xers tutor in public schools. They seek out jobs counseling school dropouts and young people who have run afoul of the law. Many actively pursue the possibility of teaching in the public education system. One young man, a star university football player, returned to his semi-rural community as a high school teacher and coach. He hopes to become a bivocational pastor in order to reach those students and their families with the Gospel. My own generation thought of engineering, law and medicine. Even the Peace Corps was a temporary assignment on the way to corporate success and the new BMW.

Personal Responsibility and Freedom

Personal responsibility and authenticity also limits personal freedom. A national survey of college freshman was very revealing. It showed that though personal freedom is a priority, students favor *limiting* it when safety or health issues arise. They favor personal searches when drugs and weapons are suspected. Eighty percent even opted for allowing employers to conduct drug tests.[86] The idea of behavior having consequence is very real to a generation that largely held the task of raising itself. The recent political swing to the right may find renewed momentum as this generation matures. Generation X will eventually shepherd the concept of personal freedom and responsibility into the PTA, community watch associations and, finally, into government.

Pluralism and Equality

Racial diversity is a fact of life in post-modern America. What the civil rights movement sought to do was engender respect and equality among races. The violence of the late 1960s choked that ideal to slow-burning coal. Affirmative action is under fire, but it did make economic neighbors of many and engendered everyday contact. Interracial marriages no longer shock anyone, and the children of the 1970s and 1980s accept racial diversity as one of the factors that make life interesting. Gen X is the most racially diverse group in the history of the United States. They are 70 percent white, 13 percent African American, 12 percent Hispanic, 4 percent Asian and 1 percent Native American. Their Boomer parents are 77 percent white.[87]

Big cities may have racial gangs and we read about neo-Nazi buffoons, but most Xers see authenticity in the idea of equality under God. The world they leave behind will probably involve some measure of racism and even ethnic enclaves. For their part, Xers will largely ignore the differences and concentrate on their own friendships indifferent to race. The search for authenticity breeds loyalties that supersede race and culture as important issues.

Multiculturalism and the Gospel

Along with multiculturalism comes a fundamental respect for all religious persuasions. Xers are not a group to accept anything without question. The major objection to Christianity rises on this front. They want to know why God would condemn sincere people of other faiths. This is no intellectual exercise to these people. I have spent half my adult life debating this issue. Only in the past few years have I met the passion I currently see in the eyes of the questioner. They are not about to accept a God who arbitrarily condemns people they love. The need for Christian apologetics is stronger than ever. This round of apologetics will be tempered with love and great patience or it won't do the job. Gen X must see it for themselves. When they do, they will make great, self-sacrificing missionaries. The sensibilities that currently render them suspicious of church and the Gospel will produce authentic and compassionate Christians.

Authenticity and the Learning Process

A lot of bad press focuses on Generation X and the learning process. They are known as "the Mr. Rogers generation," "the no-attention-span generation," and "the MTV generation." It is true that they grew up in front of television sets. True, also, that they read far less than their predecessors. While this doesn't make them lazy or mindless (consider who parked them in front of the TV in the first place), they do learn differently than any generation alive today.

Linear Thinking vs. Random Learning

I think linearly, Xers do not. Having rebelled at the idea of reading in the first grade, I was caught and put into an intensive reading program in the second grade. The plan was simple. The teacher called my mother into school and assigned her the task of reading with me for 30 minutes every day. It was only a few months before I was reading with the best of them, and I continue to devour books with all the obsession of an addict. My wife and I modeled my mom's behavior with our kids and they are both readers. Most of their friends are not. Linear thought patterns come from exposure to books. Television should be linear, too. Linear logic on TV evaporated with the advent of that wonderful device, the remote control channel surfer. It is possible to watch three or four programs at once and gather data from all of them. I know this because my children taught me. It is also possible to hold a Bible study that operates on three subjects at the same time. One subject is as boring to these people as one channel, which is almost as boring as reading. These young people aren't illiterate or uninterested, they are bored by our presentation of material.

Too authentic to put up with boredom, they simply don't show up. The idea of rapid, multiple input didn't stop with television. Consider PCs, video games, and the 'Net. Information is available at rates unheard of in the childhood of any Boomer alive. Technology defines the processing of ideas. Michael Dell, the Gen X founder of Dell Computers says, "People my age grew up knowing that computers are our friends."[88] The way they think and learn should have an impact on the way we teach God's word and structure church. Meetings should move faster, contain less identifiable liturgy, involve technology and excitement. They should also offer practical, applicable truth.

Not Necessarily Useful Knowledge

I recently discussed this idea of learning processes with a group of Gen Xers. One 30-year-old Ph.D. candidate told me: "We learn reactively and quickly. We know a lot of stuff and we are not dumb. But the stuff isn't necessarily useful to the workplace or to us. We've been provided the tools in school and through the media but they don't necessarily connect with reality. At work we are in trouble because what you know has to connect with what is." This is a cry for truth that connects to the world in which he lives. Gen X is willing and able to learn what it takes to make home and family function well. They are even interested in eternal values, they just want those values taught in a way that relates them to reality. It all has to stay interesting and remain terribly pragmatic or it just won't seem authentic.

During the same discussion, a young architect chimed in: "We're full of information, probably half of it useless. You ask a Gen Xer about a whole range of subjects and he has information available. But today there is no interaction between generations. I don't relate to my grandfather and what he did. I wasn't taught any intergenerational consequences. We never learned the big picture. Maybe the value-deprived Boomers went a generation without society breaking down, but we'll never make it. They rejected absolutes and went with the experiences of their fathers. We have less to go on. We may not make it."

A Ball in Our Court

We who have tasted of God and of life have a grave responsibility to "get real." There is a generation waiting for us to reveal to them the deep things of God. They want to know about God and ethics, God and sex, God and love, God and raising kids, God and heaven or hell. Get to know a few of them and you'll find the list of questions is endless and sincere. They want to know how to hold together the world we are passing on to them. Their concept of authenticity demands that they hold out for truth that fits their world. They will never settle for pat answers that meet the needs of the teller. Those of us who hold those answers and are willing to step across a line into another world are in for a great time.

15

Building Bridges

We all seek personal significance. Few people intentionally throw away their one shot at a meaningful contribution in this life. We may not strive for position, power or fame. But, we would all like a stab at "greatness" as I once heard it defined.

I had the good fortune to sit under Elmer Towns in a graduate course with a title that sounded somewhat inflated. The series title: "Greatness in Ministry." He defined a great man as one who affected the world more than one hour's travel time away from his home and who left a mark on people's lives two generations away from his own. Dr. Towns clarified our objections to striving for greatness when he reminded us that Jesus called us to greatness through servanthood.

Our most significant endeavors are those that result in greatness. They are those few contributions that will outlive us without succumbing to neighborhood blight. The common link between them is an investment in other people. I once read that not much which is made of wood, hay or stubble is of any long-term significance.

As a midlife Boomer, I am searching for links to significance in my own life. I find my life echoing Bob Buford's descriptives of a man at half time in the game of ministry.[89] For me, the move into significance is that of depositing my experience into someone else's account. Much as a good man leaves an inheritance for his children and grandchildren, I feel I must leave an endowment to those who follow me in the Lord's work. I intend to live the rest of my life as a bridge to the next two generations.

Are You Bridging to Jesus?

Jesus is Lord of the Church. But too often He isn't the Lord of *our* churches. We monumentalize our ministries, protect our egos and look carefully after finances. In the near term we look pretty good but one day we will face the Master. He will have some hard questions about the "talents" left in our possession.

We bridge to Jesus when His Kingdom predominates over our own. We must regularly forswear the ownership of His church that we so easily usurp. We prefer comfort, He holds out for tension on the growing edge. We are true Kingdom seekers whenever we embrace that tension.

Building to Jesus involves a crucifixion. When I was young, I died to my planned career in architecture. The cross in my life was a call into ministry. I envisioned a life of sure misery, but I said "yes." The rewards have been significant. A year or so ago, I faced another cross. I was called to die to those treasured rewards and take up an uncertain future with another generation of young people. As I get to know more and more of them, I am beginning to feel the Master's love for them. I've built a new bridge to His heart as I reach out to a generation that He loves.

Are You Building Personal Bridges?

This morning I was up very early working on this manuscript. A mainland friend called from Maui where he is vacationing. We spoke about this project and he thanked me for the effort. He expressed the need to reach out to Generation X in the large Boomer church where he is an elder. He grew up in the excitement of the Jesus Movement and wants to see another revival. He told me how difficult it is for the younger people in his church to "know what we are all about and to learn the things we know about the Lord . . ." With a heavy heart he pointed directly to the problem we face. What he did *not* see was that we must know them first. We can't expect Xers to get to know us and our mission any more than we can ask Laotian immigrants to do the same. We must build bridges to them on their turf. Our immediate job is to know them and their concerns. Only after we erect this bridgehead can we expect to infuse them with our Gospel. They will become change agents among us before we can become the same to them.

Friendship

The easiest way to build bridges is by developing a few significant friendships. I began this by leading a study group in my living room. That evolved into a very relaxed, food-filled evening every Sunday in our auditorium. We moved from the intimacy of a friendship into the structure of a successful potpourri of food, rock music, computer graphics and apologetics. It couldn't have happened without the hours spent getting to know them and their take on the world. I still go to movies with a core group about once a month after our Sunday evening meeting. We sit around and drink coffee afterward, and I listen to their comments on the film. I am trying to spend time in their world.

Focus Groups

Focus groups can produce lots of information while building bridges. While they should never take the place of friendships, they are great supplementary tools. We put together a monthly group called the "E-Team," where "E" stands for excellence. The three Boomers and three Xers drink lots of coffee while discussing their observations with our office manager who is a member of Generation X. Communication processes seem more important than execution to these people, and they provide some pretty insightful clues to our future.

Demonstrate a Willingness to Listen

A willingness to change habits is important or the bridges will break under the load of the relationship. The changes are subtle and have more to do with listening and hearing than overt behavior. They laugh at my humor which they consider "geeky." Once they caught me trying to dress like them. They thought it was a funny thing to do. They didn't really appreciate my efforts in the clothing department. They want me to remain a middle-aged man who loves them. What they do appreciate is my willingness to spend time with them. They appreciate my knowledge of history and love to hear stories about the "old days." When those stories enhance their understanding of the Bible, I become a very valuable commodity. The adjustments we are learning draw tears of laughter when I get to share my stories, often tears of sadness when I hear theirs.

Above all, I've learned to respect their cry for authenticity. This can't be faked or they walk away. Often, I have to simply hold back and let them talk. They may feel very critical of some program of ours or something going on in the larger community. The problem is that we speak two different languages. Their criticism is most always focused on that ethereal need to be "real." While I get caught up in systems or bottom-line results, they are concerned with process and integrity. If I listen long enough I earn the right to speak into their lives, and we are beginning to make a pretty good team.

I have also come to see that any ministry of future significance requires their input from the beginning. Authentic leadership of Generation X must ultimately come from one of their own. All my bridge building with a few individuals is useless if it does not keep the idea of indigenous leadership at the forefront.

How Do You Build Leadership Bridges?

A well-established leadership corps is the key to the success of any organization. We need to include Generation X leadership to ensure the ongoing success of what must necessarily be multi-generational congregations. We also need to prepare for rapid church growth, laying the groundwork for planting mono-generational churches. The process of disciple making or mentoring is a little different with Gen X than it was with our generation. It is that change of pattern that we must address in building leadership bridges.

Keep It Highly Relational

Mentoring has always been a relational process. It will be

more so with Generation X. Food figures largely into any plan to reach these people. Coffee shops at major bookstores are an earmark of their generation and say much about their learning processes. They enjoy studying and learning with friends. The successful mentor is the person who can win the position of supportive parent in this friendship. At times this involves indulging humor and language shocking to you but normal to them. Other situations will call you to function as the one person close enough to confront them when they've stepped across the line. When contemplating my relationship with Xers, I think about Paul and John Mark. Frustration gave way to a broken relationship. One generation's definition of faithfulness disqualified another's. I don't want to squander the opportunities I have with these people. Patience and commitment are crucial as I work at these relationships.

The Importance of Books

I involve books in everything I do as a mentor. When I die, those Xers will probably quote my favorite homegrown proverb on my tombstone: "If you ain't reading, you ain't leading." My staff and I only train people who are already involved in service ministry and then we assign homework as a basic foundation for any discipling process. Not given to filling in blanks, I use reading material that has shaped my own life. They read my favorite authors and we get together to discuss whatever they felt God spoke to their heart through the book. Since the book is already a treasure to me, they sense the sharing of souls when we discuss it. This approach has proven much more successful than our previous, more structured attempts. The friendship and pseudo-parenting build a strong foundation under a house of knowledge.

In our church we maintain a "loose-tight" approach to decisions. I maintain a very strong hold over basic values by the selection of books we read or Scripture we study. This tight control over values makes way for a very loose hold on decisions about ministry. I want people to feel ultimate responsibility for any area they oversee. I try to stay out of their business even if I sense they are making mistakes. I would far rather allow them to make mistakes and correct them "after the game." I don't want to panic them on the field when it comes to basic ministry decisions. This approach appeals to Xers with their sense of independence and penchant to look out for themselves.

Ease of Correction

The whole idea of correction is important and especially so with a generation raised without much parental input. I warn new leaders that I will bluntly address pride, dishonesty, and other relational misbehavior. I will also address failure to keep appointments or faithfully execute tasks. I want them to know that these issues will always lay right on top of the table and that we won't dance around them. This open atmosphere, even when we meet as a group, allows us to keep the air pretty clear. We confront an issue and quickly move on. I don't want to foster an atmosphere of vindictiveness. Judgment errors are different. Because they involve no sense of blame, we can afford longer discussions. We may spend all night dissecting a decision gone wrong and reconstructing possibilities we might face in the future. Mistakes are learning opportunities, we remember them well. Sin is different, it merits a reprimand and is quickly forgotten.

Hands on the Ministry

Hands-on training is very important with Generation X.

This is true for two reasons. The first is their relational approach to everything. They have been entertained to a point of detriment. Entertainment and lectures bore them equally. They desire personal involvement with the reality of the Gospel. The second call for hands-on experience involves their tendency to see themselves as peers to everyone else. They want to partner with me rather than sit at my feet. I find that a person who took a swing at ministry is very open to teaching about why he struck out or hit a home run. Whether he had success or failure doesn't seem to matter. He will be open to the post-mortem including all the reading and discussion that go with it.

The wonderful result of this approach is that it involves less fun and games in our programs and more spiritual output. They would rather pray for people than attend concerts. Building a house or cleaning a highway is more impressive than a church beach party. A mission trip handing out tracts is better than one where they paint buildings and go sightseeing. Tutoring second graders offers opportunity to share the Gospel with the parents of the children. With this generation, community service results in evangelism. We don't need famous people giving testimonies. That turns them off. They desire personal involvement and manage to fill in the blank spaces with the Gospel.

How to Build Congregational Bridges?

Rapid change without proper education most often spells disaster. I find that "Why?" is a far more important question than "What?" Recently, a couple of church planting officials from another denomination flew to Honolulu to discuss our model for raising up new congregations. Their questions all focused on the things we do. I kept answering their "what" questions with "why" answers, much to the consternation of us all. They really did need to look at our methods. But, methodology without well-understood reasons behind every move confuses and angers the people in the pews.

A Renewed Philosophy of Ministry

Focusing on a new target group within your congregation requires a renewed philosophy of ministry. Spending personal time with young leaders can teach you how to reach their peers. Now, your job is to educate the congregation. The old wineskins must stretch a little to include the new generation. The things you learn from Xers, contextualized within the biblical values of the congregation, provide a bridge to the future of the church. The whole congregation must understand that bridge and be willing to cross it together. If the senior leadership teaches philosophy well enough, implementation grows naturally from congregational unity.

Dispelling Stereotypes

Stereotypes separate people. Love and understanding unite them. We needed to pull the generations together before trying to lay new strategies. I began this process by illustrating my sermons with stories gleaned from the lives of Xers. A series on vision and stewardship included Generation X as a major target group. We showed a videotape summarizing much of this book at a church-wide leadership training event. In each case, we presented our young people as who they are, not the slackers of media fame. I began making jokes about my grey hair and their often-changing hair colors. My goal was for Builders and Boomers to accept Generation X as a valid piece of the pie. I wanted them to value what is good in these kids.

A Bible series on love and relationship provided a format to display some of the very strong positives this generation has to offer. Another stewardship series provided an opportunity to challenge Boomers to invest their considerable skills in the rising generation. That series opened the door for specific ministries where volunteers teach their life skills to younger people. We began to see ourselves as a diverse unity. Each generation exhibits an assortment of strengths and weaknesses. We possess very different values and experiences, yet we can fit well together in the Body of Christ. When the Boomers began reaching out to Xers, they were amazed at their loyalty and the strength of their relationships. They saw something of value missing in their own lives. When they learned from those they sought to teach, stereotype melted into love and we were on our way.

Create a New Worship Paradigm

Tradition is wonderful stuff. It guides decisions and provides a sense of belonging. Without it, life would lose its luster. Each generation, within each culture, builds its own set of traditions and attendant memories. Whenever we cross generations or cultures, we encounter a clash of traditions. Shifting paradigms can allow a person from one tradition to see clear to value another person's tradition. Such a shift is necessary to prevent war in a church bent on change.

Music and clothing are lightning rods of church tradition. Both are largely a matter of taste. No one can defend an attack on another's form or outward appearance from Scripture. Service format might be another hot spot in some churches, but still takes a backseat to music and dress. The desire to serve a crowd with dissimilar tastes leads to an inevitable question: Do we create separate services for separate generations, or do we attempt blended services? By blended services, I mean those where we try to mix music and clothing styles while we mix generations.

You can't beat separate services for functionality. The ability to do a thing well is not usually a product of compromise. A service focused toward the Builder generation will include lots of hymns and a liturgical feeling. The Boomers are into drama, colored lights and a smooth flow to the music. Generation X dresses grungy, restyles music from other eras, loves a message with a hard edge and worships God in their own unique way. To mix venues is to deny everyone the purity of experience they crave. This becomes more significant whenever evangelism is allowed into the picture.

Blended services provide a different benefit. They allow for a family feeling and often allow a heritage transfer by osmosis. This approach usually appeals the most to whichever generation will control the agenda. They have the least to lose when compromise decisions are made.

The idea of separate services targeting different age groups is not foreign to our congregation. We learned improvisation by operating for a decade and a half in a public school. Our nine year trek toward a building permit proved a blessing. Continually pressed for space, we multiplied services and launched new churches to prove faithful to the Great Commission. We currently hold six meetings each weekend with a different worship band and a different focus in each. We preach roughly the same sermon in each service, although it may be preached by three different pastors.

To us, the idea of intentionally blended services is a little radical. We currently blend our venue at each of the larger Sunday morning services, though they are still Boomer focused. Friday and Sunday evenings are Generation X events with food and fellowship following rock music and pointed Bible teaching. Blue jeans are proper attire. Saturday nights are for the Millennial generation and they get the facility for a hang-out after their church service. On Sunday mornings, bright and early, we service the Builder crowd. Though I am a Boomer, the Builder music, clothing and loving atmosphere give me a great sense of security.

You need to ask yourself which setup would be best for your particular church. Larger churches may be better suited to make the decision for separate church services. Smaller congregations feel a stronger need for unity. They may find it easier to build a separate service by calling it by another name. If your people are willing to compromise enough to embrace each other's worship styles, perhaps a blended service would be best. A word of caution: Few individuals are willing to fully embrace someone else's music and tradition.

Willing to Cross Your Bridges?

What can you expect when you attempt to bridge the gap between generations? We always live with at least four generational cohorts in significant numbers. Switching from a format dominated by one generation (plus children) to a mode that meets the needs of all four offers real challenge. It will trigger changes outside our master plan.

Lose a Few

Moving into the role of a bridging church will cost you some members. Some of them will be great people with wonderful potential. This kind of pruning always provides opportunity for fresh growth, if handled properly. The blended service is possibly most vulnerable to loss as people feel the tension of having to share worship with someone else's tradition. The separate service approach will pull people from existing meetings into new ones. This leaves some people unable to accept the change and a few will leave. It is important to anticipate these possibilities so the leadership team doesn't lose morale.

Gain a Lot

Any change that allows the church to focus more specifically on the needs of people will bring new people into membership. Simply closing the back door to those who didn't quite fit generates church growth. An extension of the closed back door philosophy is a wider front door. When people feel that their church specifically meets their needs, they get excited. The excitement of fulfilled needs quickly spills over into conversations in the workplace. Evangelism is the product of *one-to-one* communication. Excited Christians beget new birth. Outsiders may never come because you pulled off such an exciting meeting or because your music appeals to their generation. They will come if your members are proud of the Lord and their church.

Whatever choice you make will be a step toward a future that is upon us whether we prepare for it or not. Generation X is here to stay. Their little brothers and sisters of the Millennium are pressing into adolescence. I guess you could say it's not a Boomer world anymore.

16

Managing Generation X

The future belongs to the rising generation. Some aggressively grab onto it. In our early 20s, we Boomers hit the streets chanting, "Never trust anyone over 30." That was just another way of saying, "We want our place at the table of leadership." Today, long past the age of 30, we still share that table with those who slid over to make room for us. It is time to invite our Generation X friends to dine with us. Unlike us, they don't clamor for a seat. We must invite them to the party or they won't come.

Hiring Generation X

One way to bring Xers into leadership is to hire them. We maintain a *hiring pool* of younger people with leadership potential. We look to them first, even while filling non-leadership positions. My former secretary is a Hawaiian man about twice my size. He is a member of Generation X. Today he is our primary backup preacher. Within a few years he plans to plant a church aimed toward his own generation. Our part-time bookstore employees are all members of our volunteer youth staff. We hired them because of their potential for pastoral ministry. Our goal is to add to their ministry skills. We know they will absorb experience and outlook from the rest of the staff. Their increased visibility also puts them in line for other positions as they open.

Promoting the Top, Hiring the Bottom

Another line on this hiring sequence is to promote from within while liberally hiring at the bottom of the pyramid. This pretty much assures successful promotions. You can reasonably predict the success of someone whose abilities you've already witnessed. Hiring at the top requires you to bet on someone you barely know. He'd better fit your church culture or his input can unleash some real damage. Hiring at the bottom is far less risky. It brings fresh ideas into the ranks at a level where little damage is possible. It allows younger voices to influence staff decisions. Your investment is oriented toward the future rather than the past. Conversely, hiring at the top freezes everyone in position and ages the organization. There are times when hiring maturity is a necessity. But, as a general practice, it tends to preserve the past at the expense of the future.

Swelling the Ranks

You can save money by swelling the ranks with lower-paid staff positions. In addition to gleaning fresh ideas, hiring at the bottom frees money for a larger staff. Promoted people work within an existing salary structure. A raise is less expensive than enticements plus moving expenses. In our church we use that financial advantage to staff more positions at the bottom of the pyramid. This brings more young people into our development systems. We win in two ways. More people are trained for pastoral ministry, and more ministry takes place.

Churches sometimes "save" money by cutting back on youth staff positions. But these are the least expensive jobs we fund. They also generate numerical growth and tithe dollars from grateful parents. Other staff positions tend toward maintenance and are much harder to justify financially. They surely don't represent an investment in the next two decades of the life of the church. More youth staff affords a larger church as well as on-the-job training for a future pastor.

We are currently assembling an educational package rewarding young, part-time staff members for longevity. The longer they stay with us, the larger percentage of their education we will finance. Our goal is to start them young in ministry, add the benefit of formal education and then watch the investment pay off in our congregation or new ones we birth.

A New Managing Style

Working with Generation X calls for Boomers and Builders to learn a new management style. Most of what I include in the next few paragraphs is gleaned from personal experience. However, I also want to call your attention to an insightful book entitled *Managing Generation X,* by Bruce Tulgan.[90] This book reflects communication issues from the other side of the generation gap. Tulgan, an Xer, surveyed members of his own generation about their experiences in corporate America. His primary message is a cry for mutual trust.

Communication

Trust is often hard to come by, especially when cultures clash and words seem to have different meanings. For example, "I'll be at a meeting" means "showing up" to your average Boomer. To an Xer it means, "I'll try to be there." This huge cause of frustration in my church staff is not a question of responsibility versus irresponsibility. It is one of communication. Xers routinely make *approximate* plans and forgive one another for not showing up. They easily roll with a good reason for the failure to appear. Boomers expect a warning when their charges don't make an event. We've had to teach the twin concepts of *prior arrangement* and *mutual reporting* to our younger staff. There are other areas of generational miscommunication. I hold up the example to make the point that we need to learn each other's language.

The Boomers on our church staff really struggled with these language lessons. For years, we imputed wrong motives whenever these communication gaps occurred. Miscommunication translated to sheer irresponsibility. The problem was magnified by a maddening tendency of the Xers to absorb a lecture without much response or even to quit the post because they couldn't measure up. We tried to see our scrappy but responsible selves in them, but they wouldn't fight back. We had to learn the patience to go over breakdowns sequence by sequence until we understood where communication broke down. Only then could we develop a set of mutual expectations that allowed work to proceed smoothly.

"Grungy" Tastes

Clothing styles have never bothered me. I am very conscious of my appearance but quite tolerant of how others look and dress. After all, I once earned the title "hippie."

Grunge-dressing Xers face no persecution in our church. Our people take pride in the ministry and look past the clothing into the heart. Grunge clothing styles won't last forever. In our culture, clothing is a symbolic vehicle identifying a person's "place" in society. As Xers grow older, their tastes will change. Remember, the hippies of the 1970s became the yuppies of the 1980s. The mission of the church is not to monitor dress but to win hearts. In our church, we pay little attention to outward appearance; however, we do hold young leaders to higher standards of the heart.

While our church is filled with people who experiment with their hair color, this does not justify the junior high pastor dying his a flaming yellow-orange color. That only causes parents to think twice before letting their kids ride in his car. The night two male youth leaders sang and danced as the "Leotards" didn't win any merit points either. They were dressed in black polka-dotted yellow tights.

Once in awhile I hear a joke that would have been strongly off color in my youth. I intervene. These people attach little sense of morality to their humor. To them, God made body functions to enhance stand-up comedy. This, too, is a learning situation. For the Xer, a little wisdom is in order. Meanwhile, Boomers need the patience to hang in and teach the lesson. My point is that no one need lose their head (either figuratively, or in the more job-oriented sense). We have learned to keep calm and work with the raw material, no matter how raw it is. Currently, a raised Boomer eyebrow will clue an Xer to have a *straight talk* with the Xer sitting next to him. The big lesson for Boomers in our church was how much the next generation needed us. We must provide information and values where their parents and schools have failed.

Paying Their Dues

Highly-opinionated leaders often accomplish great things. Do you remember Winston Churchill or Douglas MacArthur? Our society tends to play toward the middle, marginalizing opinionated people. We opt for the graduate with the best grades and can't understand why he can't color outside the lines. We ask for creativity but hire safety. Take heart, Generation X is here. They *nearly all* color outside the lines. Problem is, they often don't know how to frame the picture.

Paying dues is not what they are about. My generation learned to pay dues in terms of respect, time on the job and credibility. After we earned our way into the hearts of management, we showed them our stuff. It was a nice arrangement and I remember it fondly. Today things are a little bit different. Generation X can't see themselves, at work, as part of a dysfunctional family. Largely self-reared, they learned to make their own decisions from an early age. They had to produce or be left out. They expect control over their environment from the first day on the job. They arrive as peers to the veterans. They compensate for this with blinding loyalty, especially in the church. The promise of the ministry is love and affection. They will go over the top *for* you, but they still think they have little to learn *from* you. They often jump into tough situations with reactive decisions that can dearly cost their boss or mentor.

I want people I mentor to patiently learn before moving to the firing line. Xers want discipleship without instruction. In their minds, they signed onto a partnership. They see the position as the authority and put their ideas right to work. Often those ideas are undeveloped and lacking in the wisdom born by experience. The partnership is vertical in my eyes, all too horizontal in theirs. No disrespect is intended on their part and they are often hurt when we hold them back while they learn. They must be taught that there are dues to pay, while my peers and I must learn that their aggressive behavior is no slight on our wisdom. Once again, conflict can become one-sided. The Xer will take heat without ever expressing his opinion to his mentor. Both his frustration and his commitment can remain obscure to the person who most wants to help him. Only much patient communication can leap this hurdle.

Setting Parameters

We recently lost a wonderful employee because we didn't set stiff-enough parameters around her schedule when we framed the job. She worked the minimum hours set forth and then took another job on the side. When our workload increased she was boxed into the other situation and had to quit our position to keep up with her other commitments. Had we more clearly spelled out the time requirements from the beginning, she would have never taken the other job. Being Boomers, we never anticipated that she would constrict her schedule without telling us first. We had no problem with her working two jobs. But we had bigger plans for her and never told her until it was too late. We would have even given her more hours had she told us she needed money. She didn't. She assumed she had been given tight parameters for her work. Boomers don't build tight parameters. At least, we didn't until we met Generation X. Now we're learning.

Two of our young employees assumed oversight of a huge revamp in a literature distribution ministry. The task was enormous and stretched on for weeks. But nobody specified how many weeks. They were sneaking into the office after hours working on the project for no pay. Their boss caught them burning out and forbade them to work more than their regular hours. He still put no parameters on the overall length of the project. They complained that he gave them a job to do but not enough hours to accomplish it. They were most angry that he didn't appreciate all the free time they offered. The dust settled when he helped them build a calendar spreading the work over three months instead of the three weeks the Xers had estimated. Parameters in place, they were happy.

Our generation wanted a goal, an occasional progress meeting, and then to be left to our own devices. Gen X wants very specific details about the goal and the boundaries surrounding them. Checkpoints and updates suggest their boss is a spy. They resent them. They check back when the goal is reached. Once they have the parameters, they assume complete freedom within the boundaries. They also assume complete freedom from *everything* outside those specified boundaries. If it isn't in the original plan it probably won't happen. This is fine if the original parameters were set by the Holy Spirit, rather than some mere pastor. However, clairvoyance is not my gift and things do change. Another problem with the Xer plan occurs when difficulty arises and the goal can't be met. They will continue with the original parameters until D-Day when they can only report failure.

The larger portion of these problems belong to Gen X. The onus is on them to learn to work within a system. Meanwhile, we Boomers must learn that we face a problem of defined boundaries, not a bunch of lazy people. Once we understand the dilemma, we can negotiate a solution. We can trade more detailed plans for regularly scheduled checkpoints, complete with hard questions about details. Simply treating Xers like we want to be treated somehow distorts the *law of love* into something that sets them up for failure. They don't want the sloppy kind of freedom that we so demanded. Theirs is the freedom of boundaries. The paradox here is that they assume freedom in day-to-day decisions, as I mentioned in the previous section, while craving boundaries for long-term projects.

Time and Overtime

Xers are very protective of their time. Given the opportunity to earn extra money by working overtime, they will often refuse. Boomers work from the opposite perspective. I put myself through college with earnings from two jobs that included more overtime money than regular pay. Through my Boomer eyes, Xers' distaste for overtime or any other drain on their personal life looks like failure to support the team. They see it differently. They are protective of relationships, and relationships take time. They want to be sure they have plenty of it available.

An example of the unpredictable need for free time is the process of "going out." Going out for many Xers involves a long process of inviting every friend they see in a given day to the movies that night. Everyone usually agrees to go and also agrees to meet at one person's house or apartment. Upon arrival they will decide which film to see and at what time. Appearing at various (non-appointed) times, they begin phoning whoever hasn't shown up. Phone calls invite more delays as the night wears on. They might make the late showing of a movie or perhaps just enjoy the experience of being together trying to contact those who didn't make it. I write this as a parent and employer who enjoys watching movies with the Xers in my life. I describe the process with their permission. The procedure incites insanity in some Boomers. But it works well for process-oriented, relationship-focused Generation X. They enjoy spending time together.

You can see why they don't like to put extra time into the job. They want predictability at work to support unpredictability in their social life. This is no function of laziness. The Bible espouses loving friendships as it does diligence in the workplace. Once our older staff members understood the value of their thinking, they could better train and manage Xers. As we began to express appreciation for their friendship needs, they immediately responded to our scheduling constraints. We now get extra time from them when they understand the importance of what we are doing. We've learned to support their stress on relationships. A circle of friends is a pseudo family to most Xers. Their loyalty and commitment to their circle comprise a practice run at a healthy home. These qualities are the building blocks of our future success in church and community.

Hug an Older Leader

Xers see mentors as surrogate parents. They often show respect by keeping their distance. Anything you or I do to overcome that distance is much appreciated by them. They often forego the love and encouragement because they don't know how to ask for it. Our staff is learning that we should initiate conversations with Xers. We even feel that we must initiate the office humor. Our goal is that they see us as approachable. We want them to feel safe asking for help on a project or advice about life. Staff outings build friendships and build trust. These range from beach days to group sporting events. We once spent a day playing laser tag in an amusement center.

We teach younger leaders to show appreciation to their

elders. The need for this is especially strong in the larger volunteer team, outside the staff. The people who faithfully laid the foundation for Generation X successes need to hear words of appreciation. Part of my management job is to teach my charges to show others that they appreciate the relationships and process that birthed their ministries. Hugging older leaders doesn't come naturally to Xers. You must teach it.

Staying Committed

Working with younger people is dangerous. One minute you are so proud of them that the buttons pop off your shirt. The next moment they embarrass you by a case of forgetfulness or through a lousy judgment call. The temptation to give up is strong at times.

Embarrassing misdeeds on the part of those I mentor try my own integrity. When their judgment goes awry, I can hold my charges responsible to the values I've taught them. Or, I can hold them accountable to the measure of someone critical of them and of me. Conflicting standards are grossly unfair. Holding our course lowers the cost of mistakes in their eyes as well as mine. My job is to defend them from the criticism of others while keeping them answerable to their lessons. A mistake made within understood parameters may occasion praise instead of scolding. Keeping the values in sight turns every failure into a classroom. This approach provides our young leaders with freedom to grow. They may make me look funny, but victory is sure if we remain committed to each other.

17

Churches for Generation X

I recently read that "There are no easy answers . . . few models . . . little resources . . . and no single place that equips people for ministry to and with Generation X. Ministering to Xers is a learn as you go process."[91] True words, but no justification for inaction. Fumbling our way forward can only lead to victory. Doing nothing invites certain disaster. This is more like a drawn out military campaign than a sales strategy. You take ground, only to lose it again. In the loss, you fall back and learn how to reclaim your earlier conquests, gaining new tactics in the process. The secret to success is relentless commitment to the learning process.

Boomers Ministering to Xers

I speak as a continual learner. For the moment, three of the four largest ministries to Gen X in Hawaii are pastored by Boomers like myself. The fourth is a church we birthed four years ago. It is pastored by a first-year Xer. All of us continue in our struggle to develop effective tools for touching Generation X. My church remains particularly committed to building an easily reproducible model. We intend to move through the transition from a church that birthed a movement of Boomer churches into one that duplicates that success in the next two generations. As I write, I can anticipate about 20 good years of active ministry for myself. My primary focus in those remaining years is to develop a cadre of Gen X churches. My end goal is to coach them forward as they begin passing the baton of leadership to Millennial generation congregations, and watch them build churches.

In his book *New Paradigm Churches,* University of Southern California religion professor Donald Miller makes the point that there had to be a Chuck Smith and a John Wimber before there could be a Bill Hybels. These Builder generation men handed off the football of pastoral ministry to a team of Boomer pastors. Those Boomers gained great yardage by planting churches specifically targeting their own generation. A parallel movement is the object of this book. If enough Boomer congregations can switch into a transition mode, we can raise a generation of leaders capable of engendering the rapid growth associated with revival.

Because Generation X values intimacy over a crowd. First glance suggests that they may never build megachurches. Faith Popcorn, a futurist, believes the choices for the future include only megachurches or small intimate *boutique* congregations. She says megachurches must operate as villages providing boutique experiences through small groups and intimate ministry settings. Her projections spell difficulty for mid-size congregations built on experiences involving the entire congregation.[92] The trend toward smaller is all the more reason to try to smother the earth with new congregations. In the next few paragraphs, I want to share some of the things we've learned in a congregation that can safely, if temporarily, boast the largest contingency of Xers in our state. At the risk of self service, I will present our church as a model because I know it best. Also, because our daughter churches are smaller versions of the mother.

Ministry Will Look Different

Ministry in monogenerational Xer churches will look a lot different than what we're used to. It will also sound different not only musically, but in teaching and leadership styles. As I write about these surface issues, I fear that my readers will misunderstand my description. I am *not* saying that we change the music and preaching to entice non-Christians into our meetings. I am simply detailing our own attempts to meet Christian Xers and their twin needs for relationship and authenticity. Little of what we do would directly appeal to an unbelieving stranger. That is not our goal. We believe in the power of face-to-face evangelism so we never try to be different for the sake of imitating the world. Our sole concern is with building up our people so they will effectively minister to their peers. We are very concerned with style and those surface issues that you would immediately notice if you visited our church. But this is not style for the sake of style. We adjusted our style to the hearts of young people we've come to know and love. They dictate our style by their approach to life.

Meeting Format

Restrictive facilities force us to spread our congregation

throughout six services each weekend. The evolution of those services is such that our evening meetings focus entirely on younger people. Both Friday and Sunday evenings are Gen X meetings while our Saturday service is home to about 150 Millennial generation high schoolers.

Each of the evening meetings involves food and a very relaxed atmosphere. Levi Strauss would be proud if he ever visited our church. We greet the people with food after work on Fridays. After the worship and preaching on Fridays and Saturdays, we turn the auditorium into a large coffee shop with card tables, sofas, big screen video, etc. The hang-out time is inexpensive, safe and very productive.

Sunday evenings are dedicated to some pretty heavy apologetics, so we lighten the atmosphere with a coffee/ fellowship break between the worship and teaching times. Preaching in these meetings is often from a stool. There is no pulpit and our preachers move around a lot. Dialogue with the audience is not uncommon during sermons. Recent experimentation dabbles with a talk show style setup. In that situation, the message delivery system is a dialogue between two people mixed with audience participation.

Preaching Style

Our preaching style is not so unique. We teach all our budding preachers to start every message with a story from their own lives or from the life of our congregation. The Gospel of Mark tells us that Jesus never taught without using parables.[93] We believe in the wisdom of His example. The parable or life-related story draws out a cynical audience. Vulnerability equates to authenticity as the speaker displays his own shortcomings or humorous life adventures. Whenever the story is the spiritual victory or struggle of a church member, the message of Scripture is on verifiable public display.

If we don't begin with a story, we pose questions to the audience. George Barna champions Socratic questions as a way of opening Generation X eyes and hearts.[94] We believe he is onto something. Some are hypothetical questions, others are meant to be answered. On Sunday evenings it is routine to pose a thoughtful question, asking the audience to answer among themselves during the coffee break. When we regather for teaching, we ask the braver members to venture their opinions in short interviews. Short, pointed and often humorous, these interviews look more like a segment from MTV than from David Letterman.

Preaching is topical in venture, expository in nature. We roam around the Bible, but mostly preach complete passages of Scripture. Generation X doesn't like to read but they enjoy synopsis of literature. Penguin Books currently enjoys huge success in condensed books. The 150 titles in their Penguin 60 Series are currently the hottest products in their entire spread. These are edited highlights of the classics. Each book is a synopsis of the literature of the ages.[95] This is less than what we might hope, but surely a link to the literature that formulated our society. Preaching can accomplish a similar purpose. My goal is to make the Bible so interesting in short form that non-readers are enticed into the full, uncut version each morning.

Spoon-fed truth in a short, fast-moving package is the goal of my preaching. Mark Twain is supposed to have observed that no sinner was ever saved after the first 20 minutes of a sermon.[96] A generation that grew up on funny Super Bowl commercials needs to hear a concise, interesting message or they will switch channels. In the interest of easy reading, we switched to the New Living Translation one week after it came out. The ease of language draws people into Scripture. Some people criticized the move as a sacrifice of accuracy. The trade off is simple, the Bible gets read more often this way. We used a modern translation before the switch. Yet many people still rave that the new Bible opened the door to personal Bible reading for the first time in their lives. I would venture to say that Gen X, raised on television, is culturally incapable of grasping the message of the older King James Version. This is cross-cultural ministry and includes all the problems associated with placing Scripture in the vernacular of the people.

We reinforce preaching with published notes. The notes are a follow-up tool for use in small groups that we call "MiniChurch." Sermon outlines and accompanying visuals also appear on a large projection video screen behind the preacher. Often as not, the visuals are humorous. Drama currently receives little attention as we view it a time consumer competing with our goal of 60-minute services.

MiniChurch

Our congregation enjoys small groups. The Baby Boomers made them the anchor of our pastoral development system. Small groups are the farm teams to the church planting major league. The man with pastoral gifts will succeed as a small group leader. In each group he builds a leadership team to replace himself as he leaves to start the next discipleship circle. If he establishes three successive groups, we feel he is worthy of further training.

Generation X seems tailored to the small group. Just watch "Friends" on television to get a feel for the small church in action. A few people sit around a living room supporting each other through life's maze. Adding a lively discussion of the sermon they all heard the preceding Sunday provides God's word as a foundation for their lives. Toss in a large dose of conversational prayer and you get what we call MiniChurch. The term is designed to reinforce a model centered on the Apostle Paul's idea of every member sharing input to the ministry.[97] The home meeting *is* a small church. The weekend meetings might be described as church conventions. We love to compare ourselves to the Jerusalem church in the second chapter of Acts. Large groups enjoyed the apostles' teaching in Solomon's porch at the temple. Smaller groups operated from house to house. For us the larger public space equates to the cafeteria of an elementary school. Cramped facilities forced a structure on the early church. That structure resulted in widespread lay leadership. Only lay leadership could have supplied the homes and teachers for a congregation serving at least 3,000 in Jerusalem. We voluntarily embrace the concept of lay leadership. Many churches do this. Our unique contribution has been the ability to use the home group as the primary tooling ground for pastoral training. In the trenches, education appeals to Generation X.

Highly relational, this generation craves both human contact and a touch from the Holy Spirit. The home meetings allow for both. We spend lots of time in prayer after discussing the weekend Bible teaching. Our goal with the sermon is to share what each one heard God saying to him or her as the pastor taught the passage. We each share what we feel we are supposed to do in response to God's voice. A simple format, yet highly accountable to friendship and mutual support. Each meeting *begins* with food, moves to Bible discussion and ends in prayer. They last about an hour and a half. For food, we ask for "leftovers" instead of a gift from the Colonel. Somehow, leftovers appeals to that cry for authenticity. People are sharing their own lives at one more level.

These groups are rife with answered prayer. Never allowing for "prayer requests," we simply listen to each other while eating and sharing God's word. During those times, people put their lives on display. Careful listening during those times guarantees that life's real issues get prayed over. Prayer is a round robin that holds out an implicit promise of further prayer. Your prayer is a promise that you will pray for that person throughout the week. This practice begets check-back phone calls and strengthens friendships. The Holy Spirit is promised whenever two or more gather. He is capable of accomplishing more in minutes than we are in weeks. The demonstration of answered prayer in MiniChurch is one of the greatest stimulators of Generation X evangelism in our church. Experience the power of God and you have something to talk about.

MiniChurches are not *self-actualization* groups. They don't resemble group therapy. They are little churches—spiritual laboratories where people test the data from the weekend lectures. Generation X is more interested in prayer and a sense of fellowship with the Lord than with the psychology that drove our churches for the past two decades. This is a generation concerned with the basics. Simplicity is their earmark.

Wider Range of Music

No discussion of church would be complete without a look at music in the worship experience. Music is as important to this generation as any other. The major difference here is the wide variety of music enjoyed by these people. Other than rap music, Generation X has no distinctive music style of its own. Perhaps true distinction lies in the willingness to borrow from other generations. Borrowed music infiltrates the worship context. Most of our congregational worship songs are written by a Boomer in our church who can't shake the 1970s. He puts Scripture to music with a *gift* that reminds you of Bob Dylan. Boomers enjoy his music, Xers love it. Our songs also range from Martin Luther's "A Mighty Fortress is Our God," to the Drifters' "Stand by Me" with its original Christian wording.

Eclectic music is a simple tool for worship to Xers. They are not as prone to polished presentation as the generations before them. A few guitars and a drum set satisfies their need for sound. Our worship teams look like 20-member rock bands. Xers in our church prefer slow worshipful songs to the fast ones appealing to a Boomer like me. Young people would rather sing songs *to* God than *about* Him. They crave His presence.

The move away from polished performance provides a nice surprise. Musical families are back. We've been delighted by a 6-year-old singing with her mommy. We were astounded by three teenaged sisters accompanied by their dad. Their tears tore at our hearts while their father gave testimony to God's grace in their family. The concept of people genetically included in a musical team is heartwarming to a generation largely self-reared. The quality occasionally suffers, but our crowd still loves it. They long for success at home and these groups reinforce their hopes. Our overly-entertained Xers can turn up their noses at a polished performance if they deem it boring. The same audience consistently offers warm adulation to any musical expression of family love in worship or ministry. They expect quality, but it must support not preempt the values they hold dear.

Concerts were a large part of my Jesus Movement past. We built our church around traveling musicians. About eight years ago we cut them off because people became bored with them. The first wave of Xers were making their presence known. Christian music promoters still prevail but the concert is a tougher venue for them than it was in the 1970s and 1980s. While concerts are out, something else is taking their place. We can punch up church attendance by announcing that a live band will perform during the coffee hour after the service. No one seems to pay much attention to the words, but they enjoy the presence of the band. Music is not a vehicle for delivering a message. Xers use it as a vehicle for bolstering relationships. They employ it as a background for conversation. Any truth caught along the way is more likely to come from the conversation than the lyrics.

Support Services

Our emphasis on the MiniChurch provides support from an up-close group of friends. The impetus is on the saints to do the actual work of the ministry. People gain skills and competence through service. In our church, competence has birthed a wide range of support ministries to and through Generation X.

As someone grows to ministering in a certain area, we throw a name on that function and a new department is added to the church. Most of these ministries are aimed at building stronger families. We have ministries dealing with anger management, personal finances, raising healthy children, freedom from drugs and alcohol, freedom from sexual addictions, literacy for children and adults, strength for single mothers, etc. The importance of all this is not endemic to Generation X or to our church. Every generation must face its problems. The underlying significance is that each ministry grew out of relationships between laypeople of a generation libeled as uncaring slackers.

Leadership Development

The advent of megachurches positioned the local congregation alongside the seminary as a developer of pastoral training.[98] This pattern for raising leaders from within local churches is both biblical and suited to the needs of today's world. Mentors fill a spot vacated by absentee. In an era of financial restraint, this notion further appeals on the basis of reduced economic strain. The concept of *learning by doing* parallels the current trend toward apprenticeship in the business community.[99] Generation X responds to peer leaders raised and in-service training as authentic.

The demand for credentials that drove many toward advance degrees in theology is foreign to this generation. Xers who paid the price are finding their credentials of little value in the workplace. Architects tend supermarket checkout lines. I know a geologist who found work as a machinist. The overwhelming number of jobs today don't require a college degree. The Bureau of Labor Statistics reports that nearly 25 percent of Gen X college or university grads hold jobs that do not match or require their degree.[100] The separation of daily reality from the credentialing process makes it easier for Xers to accept a pastor who was once trained as a carpenter or pharmacist.

Gen X pastors reject the notion of pastor as recruiter of a professional staff designed to pull off high-quality programs. Instead, they embrace the role of head coach who trains assistants to equip laypeople to do the work of the ministry.[101] This fits my experience in ministry training. We see the whole church as a training ground. Not everyone ascends to the top but each individual should rise some distance within the leadership pyramid. Each person on the team is responsible to bring a few disciples a little further in his steps toward the Master.

All ministry in our church branches out from our MiniChurches. The MiniChurch leader and his apprentices meet twice a month with a staff member to discuss a book they have read in concert on their own time. The staff member—himself a product of this system—is involved in a similar dialogue with myself and the rest of the paid staff at our weekly meetings. This simple tool provides the backbone of educational support for all ministry in our church. We do run seminars and specialized programs pointed toward various specific areas of ministry. These are closed to anyone not actively participating in leadership. We train recruits. We do not recruit through training. This works so well that we have started well over 100 daughter and granddaughter churches in 25 years. More than 90 percent of those pastors remain in the ministry today. Only a half dozen of those we sent out had any professional training outside the local churches prior to launch. Many of these people go on to seminary after planting the church they pastor. We encourage further education but sincerely believe in the mentoring process as the gateway to ministry.

One potential church planter is a university graduate who says he hates to read. But he created a problem in his *discipleship group* by finishing books weeks before the rest of his team. We were laughing about this one day and I asked him why he did it. He told me that he was "doing the ministry" and needed all the help he could get. As books became practical to him he could not put them down. Perhaps Generation X is practical where they have been called lazy. This new (2,000-year-old?) training paradigm seems designed with them in mind.

Church Planting

New churches need certain resources to get off the ground. Less money in the economy spawns a cry for creativity. God can help us stretch resources as He did for the first-century church at Philippi.[102] One avenue is that of teaming one generation with another. Boomer congregations are entering the years of financial ease. Our kids are moving into adulthood and our refinanced mortgages are easier to handle. We can join the next generation as a major supplier of the monies necessary to start churches. Intergenerational generosity isn't our only hope. The horizon blazes with cost-saving ideas that bear watching.

Another In-Service Advantage

The idea of pastors trained through other pastors in local churches has immense cost benefit to the local church. It saves more than tuition money. This approach allows the zealous layperson to remain in service to his local church. The uprooting of seminary students dilutes the strength of the volunteer team that raised them. The loss ultimately translates into dollars. A church that regularly sends people to seminary requires more paid staff than if it did not. Moving and lost job costs incurred by students are another economic factor ultimately affecting our churches.

Bivocational Operating Capital

A second step back into biblical church planting provides a further economy. Bivocational church planters are now the norm in some settings. These men and their families bring a huge benefit of operating capital to their churches and to those who send them. They stretch resources in a time when thinner reserves might preclude ministry. The odd thing for a Boomer to understand is the acclaim this idea has in Generation X circles. Their caution toward new endeavors renders this halfway step appealing. Many desire the independence provided by a job outside the church. Another appeal is the idea of authentic ministry at an authentic pace. They know they needn't drive the church toward growth in order to feed their families. Whatever the cause, talk to an Xer and you will find a person unafraid of bivocational church planting. A little over half our church planters are bivocational at the outset. Judging from the half dozen men on deck, that percentage will soon increase.

Mission Churches

The third cost saver is wholly new to me. This is a mission church where the pastor remains an active member of the mother congregation for an indefinite period of time. Rented facilities and an off-schedule service time promise to put more people into pastoral ministry at a faster rate than ever before. We started one church in this manner and anticipate another within the next few months. That congregation will operate on Saturday evenings in a borrowed building. The pastor will continue in our church and its training venues for as long as he chooses. This will afford easy contact with more experienced members of our staff, including myself. His current MiniChurch will remain a unit of our congregation while they function as a core of the new congregation. We believe their loyalty will drift toward the new church as their schedule becomes tiring. The bivocational pastor will go the extra mile. We'll supply music teams in the beginning and cover whatever costs they incur for six months or so. They will collect and keep their offerings, including those of the people involved in both congregations. The cost savings here cannot be measured in terms of money as much as in *risk*. Unsevered ties at home make an aborted church plant far less costly. We can learn from the pastor's experience, retool him and help him launch another attempt. Holding tighter to our relationships through the planting process appeals to the ever-cautious Xer.

Now Generation Churches

Wonderfully written articles about Boomer congregations can put us to sleep. I enjoyed one such recent article in the *Atlantic Monthly,* but I struggled with the title. Entitled "Welcome to the Next Church," the article provided an exciting profile of megachurches successfully evangelizing Boomers. It included only one reference to Xers. Both the slant and title of that article could take the spotlight off the future.[103] Boomer congregations are not the "next" church. They are becoming *past*-generation churches. *Now*-generation churches are rare and largely comprised of Generation X. The *next* generation is the Millennial cohort who currently spend their days in elementary and high school classrooms. If we sleep on our successes, we will soon preside over emptying buildings. Boomers are already pricing condos in retirement communities. If we effectively raise leaders and start "now" generation churches, someone will be around to start those "next" generation churches. The fields only grow whiter . . .

18

Another Perspective on Evangelism

Generation X is the title of a book by Canadian writer Doug Coupland. An Xer himself, he writes with unique insight to the needs and feelings of his generation. In his book *Life After God* he writes, "Now—here is my secret: I tell it to you with an openness of heart that I doubt I shall ever achieve again, so I pray that you are in a quiet room as you hear these words. My secret is that I need God—that I am sick and can no longer make it alone. I need God to help me give, because I no longer seem capable of kindness; to help me love, as I seem beyond being able to love."[104]

Coupland speaks well for his peers. Love is the missing ingredient in our country today. From home to work to school to freeway, we've forgotten how to love our neighbor. Only love for God can lay the foundation for love of fellow man. Without God, we are faced with a Darwinian ethos of competition for the gene pool. Evangelism that works must address the love issue above all others. The redemption story is foremost a story about the love of God. We must remember that a program of evangelism is not the issue. Reconciling individual people to the God who loves them is the need of the hour.

Why Do We Need New Methods?

Old methods can't work with Gen X because the audience thinks so much differently than those that came before. The old methodology is simply a package of cultural tools for teaching an eternal and unchanging truth. The message is decidedly different from the messenger in each ensuing generation. Here are 10 Gen X characteristics we must keep in mind as we communicate the love of God to this generation:

Not Intimidated by Hell

In the 1970s we brought hundreds of kids into the Kingdom with a movie called *A Thief in the Night*. We'd rent an auditorium and scare them into salvation with thoughts of missing the rapture and roasting in hell. Today's kids have gone through so much hell, personally or vicariously, that they aren't scared by the real thing. Some simply don't believe in an afterlife. Others toughened by their own experiences are willing to take their chances.

Not Satisfied with Abstract Faith

Complicated *formulas* are unimportant and unbelievable to this generation. An intellectual approach to a distant, dusty God does nothing to solve the AIDS crisis or feed starving children. Xers cannot be satisfied unless love and feeling enter the salvation portrait. This *feeling* must result in

Christians producing answers to the pain Xers see all around. They want to witness the reality of the *second* great commandment.[105] Whenever we reduce our message to mere formulas, they turn a deaf ear to our message.

Won't Go with the Flow

I once asked my (then) 22-year-old son why he and his buddies would have nothing to do with our church's singles ministry. He said, "Dad, when you're my age, you don't want a marital status." That was an insightful answer. Xers reject any ideas of participating in *movements* or official groupings. The idea behind the tag "Generation X" is that it divorces them from any label applied to them by Boomers. The worst of these identifiers was the term "Baby Busters" which categorized them in light of another generation. My daughter told me she best likes the term "No-name Generation."

Not Moved by Altar Calls

Very suspicious of manipulation, this generation is immune to the very idea behind an altar call. They tend to share ideas among themselves and build a philosophy for living a little here, a little there. These lonely yet emotionally detached, over-entertained people will not move in a herd. During the Jesus Movement, I once watched a man move an entire auditorium full of young men to an altar of evangelism. His secret—he challenged them to "Stand up and be a man for Jesus." A year ago I saw the same appeal reap 1,500 sullen stares.

The Most Cynical Generation in History

Cynicism is an endearing trait among a group raised in the glare of the media. They've been hyped by the best of all time. State-of-the-art messages teach them to merely turn off the messenger unless they experience the product. Both my kids shop much more slowly and thoroughly than my wife or myself. They make friends in the process and those friends help them with their decisions. Often those friends point them in a better direction than they had planned. Unwilling to trust a slogan about Jesus, today's young adults want to see the results first in someone they know. They want to see and handle God in the lives of others before they buy in.

Less Pre-exposed to Evangelism

A decade before they were born, people stopped attending church because it was "the right thing to do." This began with the Builder who birthed the first 10 years of Generation X. In spite of the Jesus Movement, overall church attendance waned while the first wave of Xers grew up. They didn't hear Gospel stories in Sunday School because they never attended. Christian overtones are missing from both the larger community and the childhood home. The Boomer return to church brought teen Xers and very young Millennials back into training. But, the damage was done. An American generation grew up with very little Bible knowledge. This vacancy disallows any substructure of truth previously taught. We must start each message or conversation from scratch. Hence, most current communication of the Gospel amounts to cross-cultural evangelism.

Not Respectful of Tradition

Tradition and social mores are out when it comes to decision making. The very thing that makes "Beavis and Butthead" so popular works against evangelism by church tradition. This has hardly been an issue since the days of the Vietnam War, but the appeal to tradition lingers in some circles. Today, very few people are moved to a decision by the beauty of a 400-year-old liturgy. I once visited a large church which sported a beautiful, stained-glass window. Their literature racks displayed seven different varieties of color brochures. The pamphlets proclaimed the glories of that window. When the church was built, the window drew the attention of several national magazines. The congregation actually grew because of that window. Still beautiful, the window is no longer a church growth tool. The Xers in your family might not even walk across the street to see it.

Don't Believe in Absolute Truth

Today's young people believe absolute truth is a myth. They disconnect the concept of creation from that of revelation. The God who reveals Himself to them would never have set standards or laws for the universe He built. Many don't believe He built it, but only operates within it. For them the idea of absolute truth is even more foreign. They search for the divine spirit, yet they reject the imposition of spiritual beliefs. This is why they have so much trouble with the concept of cross-cultural missions. To them, rescue from the fires of hell takes a back seat to politically correct ideas about cultural religions. Xers won't appreciate the Gospel without solid answers to their defining question, "How can God send sincere people to hell?"

Fashionable Skeptics

It is more fashionable for Xers to remain skeptical than to commit to a concept. To question authority and assumptions comes second nature to Generation X. Any new idea is wrong until proven right. Coupled with their distaste for linear logic, this makes for slow debates. One positive merit in this skepticism is the tendency to stay away from groups like those of our generation who drank the spiked punch at

Jonestown.

Take the Longer Road

We may arrive at the same destination, but the road for Xers is more circuitous. Unused to linear thought, they will interrupt conversations with a thousand questions and slide down a hundred alleyways. The attractive side of this is their ability to hold onto several thoughts at once. Their learning patterns may be spotty, but they are quick. What makes these patterns unattractive is the difficulty it presents to the linear communicator. Preaching, Bible study, even late-night discussions over coffee require heavy retooling from Boomers who care about Xers.

What Seems to Work

A few weeks ago I spoke on the evangelism of Generation X at a pastors conference. One woman looked puzzled throughout the session. Afterward she asked me, "What is so different about what you are saying from what we did when we were younger?" She was a Boomer, saved through the work of street evangelists during the Jesus Movement. The real point of her question was that I was saying nothing she didn't already know. She was correct. Successful ministry is not exotic. Most of what I've discovered in our own church or in other ministries fit the profiles found in the Book of Acts. Periodically, we stray into mechanics. The Holy Spirit then hauls us back into *relationship* as the principal medium for a message of reconciliation.

Marketplace Evangelism

The popular Christian alternative band *Jars of Clay* plays in bars. An article I read featured a Christian woman complaining about having to bring her kids into a bar to hear Christian rock musicians.[106] A punk rock group in our church plays in bars in an effort to target the other musicians and employees. They had the courage to rock the University of Hawaii campus in an effort to draw a crowd for an evangelistic rally but seem lost when playing in a Christian concert. These guys play regularly in worship bands so the church setting is not the problem. They are simply more at ease evangelizing on non-Christian turf. The word "authenticity" cropped up in a conversation with them about this phenomenon. They feel they are taking the Gospel where it belongs which is outside of the church building.

I was impressed with a young pastor who told me a few weeks ago that he went to *Borders*, the megabookstore in his city. They agreed to let him organize a reading group on the "Spiritual Journey." He won't preach or lead a Bible study. Instead, he will lead people into a number of books about spirituality, including some by C.S. Lewis. Ministry in the marketplace works for Generation X.

High Profile Events

Parachurch events are easier to spot than local churches because they tend to assume a higher profile. Three thousand young people attending a concert or 40,000 at a Jesus festival get written up in the Christian music industry press. Three hundred Generation Xers meeting in an industrial building doesn't get as much notice. While the local church is the backbone of *the* Church, these larger gatherings can and do contribute to the overall growth of the Kingdom.

I want to draw a careful distinction here between evangelistic events like those of the 1950s and modern parachurch worship and teaching events. Since Generation X is resistant to hype and manipulation, they *dutifully* manifest grave difficulty with the machinations of arena evangelism. By contrast, a close-up view of thousands of Christians in worship or training becomes an opportunity to test drive the Gospel message. The ability of Promise Keepers to pull in a Gen X audience and produce long-lasting conversions testifies to this sensation. I interviewed several new converts after a recent Promise Keepers Rally in Honolulu. They were "blown away" by the sincerity of the men sitting around them. One very young Xer actually asked a mid-life Boomer he had never met to go forward with him during an altar call. They probably wouldn't have shown up for a "salvation show." The reality of Christian men at worship was interesting and served as a kind of "bait" for the event.

The evangelistic rock concerts of the 1970s drew crowds willing to listen to the novelty of Christian music to a rock beat. This kind of novelty isn't much of a draw to a crowd numbed by fireworks and bungee jumpers at secular rock concerts. The reality of worship and warm Christian fellowship can and does draw nonbelievers, one at a time.

Christian Gimmicks

Bumper stickers and T-shirt slogans may be insipid but they are good conversation starters. These gimmicks can result in evangelism. Many people have come to Christ by virtue of the question, "What's that on your T-shirt?" When Andrew told Peter about the Messiah, one-on-one conversation qualified as the primary tool for evangelism. Weak unto themselves, gimmicks do stimulate conversation. In our last congregational survey, several people described a simple bumper sticker as their first pointer toward Jesus. Follow-up research showed that in every case, they already knew someone from our church and the bumper sticker led to face-to-face discussions of our church and the Lord. The gimmicks are just gadgets. However, the questions they spark can move people toward relationally-oriented evangelism.

Prayer

Recently, a group called Joshua Force spent a day in front of the Washington Monument in the nation's capitol. Their mission was to offer "free prayer" to anyone who wanted it. Some of the 20 young people circled the crowd supporting their teammates with prayer. The others stood under a sign, announcing their intent. Curiosity paid off. A crowd soon gathered and people lined up for prayer. No one reacted negatively all day. As many as 15 people lined up at a time for prayer. Several people accepted Jesus Christ as their Savior that day.[107] The street scenes in Judea must have looked much the same as the apostles offered relief in the name of the Master.

We teach our congregation to pray whenever the situation calls for it. Members might ask permission to pray for a co-worker's problems. They usually offer to pray in their own home during personal prayer times. The person being prayed for isn't even present. Braver people will pray on the spot, especially in an emergency. Generation X welcomes prayer. People feel flattered that a friend or co-worker would pray for them. Flattery means little, but answered prayer draws people toward God. This is as near to the lives of the apostles as anything I have ever seen in personal evangelism. Xers who taste the Spirit will seek a relationship with Him.

What Can We Do?

Paul said he was all things to all men.[108] His desire was to win some. He won an empire with that flexibility. His sermon to the worshipers of an "unknown god" stands as a call to flexible, creative communication with Generation X. The past three decades called for logical, linear presentation of Scripture. In the recent past, people largely *thought* their way into a relationship. A person required intellectual conviction before experiencing spiritual conversion and the relationship we call church. Today the tides have turned. Xers work into new thought paradigms *through* friendship. Intellectual understanding and commitment to the Gospel often follows conversion. Conversion occurs when the presence of the Holy Spirit and the love of a trusted friend intersect. Love leads the way.

Major in Love

My wife volunteers as a reading tutor in a local elementary school. Her experience is multiplied in countless others who identify their primary job as giving hugs and rewards. The teacher tells her that the children who read best are always those best loved at home. Those who lack it, lap it up on Tuesday and Thursday mornings during those reading sessions.

Raised without adequate parental input, Generation X responds well to a Heavenly Dad who loves unconditionally. Words emphasizing His love and patience meet damp eyes and open ears. The thought of a "super father" who takes time to hear every cry, touches young people in the center of their loneliness. His power to heal and forgive appeals to the abused and spiritually wounded. Offer enough spiritual hugs and they will fall in love with the Lord of heaven and earth.

Friendship Evangelism

Make friends with Xers outside the church and you will lead people to Christ. I sometimes go sit in coffee shops dedicated to grunge clothes, old sofas and piles of magazines. Whenever I do this, I am amazed at the kindness shown to a middle-aged preppie. Absolutely out of my own context, I relate through smiles and words of encouragement. The love goes both ways. The seeds of friendship grow slowly, but I have several friends whose names I don't yet know. We just know each other. Some know me as "that pastor from Hope Chapel." That is enough for now. Patience must prevail lest they feel manipulated. Pain will provide open doors for deeper conversation, and these kids major in pain. Over the long haul, love will pave the way for a trickle of converts. Discipling the converts could turn the trickle into a flow. The hard part for me is remembering that these are people, not evangelistic goals.

A Softer Sell

George Barna suggests the possibility of *negative pressure* toward evangelism. He proposes the use of questions to draw Xers into dialogue on their own terms. Using Socrates as a model he defines this teaching method as "Socratic evangelism."[109] The idea is to lead the learner to a desired truth through his own opinions. Should the student reverse the process by asking questions, he invites declarative truth or another set of questions from the teacher. Even modest attempts at this appeal to Generation X. People like spending time with others who value their opinions. Socratic evangelism mixes together common sense, basic assumptions, and Xers' love for opinionating. If you try this, the least thing that can happen is for you to gain a living room full of new friends. Jesus never used the term "Socratic evangelism," but this use of questions is one of the foundational communication skills of the New Testament.

Be as Accepting as Jesus

The presence of *former* homosexuals in our lay leadership teams signals that our church is open to people struggling with that problem. An attitude of love toward people suffering the guilt of abortion salts the earth toward saving the lives of other babies. Love merits a hearing with nonbelievers who operate by the rules of this world. Generation X wars against the imposition of values. Churches crusading against secular sin turn them off. For this reason, Paul's injunction against judging outsiders becomes an implement for evangelism.[110] Our choice to love those hated by some Christians builds bridges to non-Christian people. We fly our flags high and they understand our view of their behavior. They also know we won't condemn them for that behavior. They may disagree with our theology but they never turn us off because of the acceptance of Jesus in our actions. Communication, love and acceptance unfetters Gen Xers in their attempts to evangelize their friends.

Stay Attuned to the Holy Spirit

Prayer for Xers will keep you in touch with the Holy Spirit. Get to know them up close and you will be driven to fasting. Immense hurts, poor economic prospects and lowered personal expectations will tear your heart into little pieces. Each piece will cry to God for a better life for them through Jesus Christ. As you spend time with these young people, they will sense your walk with God in word and in character. Your friendship with God will attract them to the Master. In your conversation, emphasize the mystical, spiritual side of your walk. Let the words "Holy Spirit" appear often on your lips. The "New Age" appeals because it offers an attractive counterfeit to the aspect of Christian life that we often hide when dealing with nonbelievers. Xers are looking for spiritual action. Xers will question you about your references to the Holy Spirit. The conversations they start will lead to the Cross.

Praying with them is better yet. Once you open conversation about the power of God, they will want to test it. Get non-Christians praying and the fireworks begin. My days of street evangelism during the Jesus Movement taught me that God loves to answer prayers offered by non-Christians. That lesson stands today. I will do almost anything to get unbelievers to pray. Loving answers from an attentive Father shock them into the Kingdom.

Is There Really Hope?

An older pastor once told me, "The person who generates the most hope in the community will have the strongest voice in the community." I've found his axiom as true among Xers as with anyone else I encounter. Our hope is Jesus Christ. We continually speak of hope for a better community through the influence of the Gospel and the hard work of our members. We've become dispensers of hope. The watching world searches for the hope that beats within our chest. The community sees us as a community of hope within the larger community. Xers in our church live the analogy. In spite of all the despair about Generation X, these young people are very capable of well-placed hope and godly dreams. Their friends *are* watching.

Discussing the prospects of Generation X, Leighton Ford quotes a friend who said, "Remember, God really is God. He's not applying for the job."[111] If God feels no despair, I have every reason to expect great results. God is the author and finisher of salvation. The passion we feel for Xers and their wounds was born in His heart. He will prevail through you and me. I expect revival as we reach out to Jesus with one hand and to our younger brothers and sisters with the other.

19

Weighing the Options

A very young man recently challenged me in a way that I would like to challenge you. He walked into my office carrying a book I wrote denoting the history of Hope Chapel.[112] He liked the book but demanded, "Where is the next *Ralph Moore* around this place?" I pointed to him and said, "He's you." That wasn't good enough.

He told me I didn't understand. He said that he was just an intern in our church. He wanted to know where the next true pioneer would come from. I pointed out one of our staff members who had just resigned to plant a church. He began with more than 400 people the first week and is laying plans for daughter churches from the outset. Again, this wasn't a good answer.

He corrected me, "You guys do everything relationally and with teams. This is great, but you had no team when you went out. Where is the guy

207

tough enough to start from scratch with no mother church? Who will knock on doors all over a city?" Then he delivered the knockout punch, "Who is strong enough to be independent of you and do what you did?" He got to me with his last statement.

Old Stories

I am forever telling others to beware of traditions and systems because they choke off revival. I perceive my ministry as a product of the last revival. I like to think the revival is alive in our church, and certainly in the Foursquare family of churches. We are growing faster than anyone else around. Our movement harvested the best of the past two revivals. We keep the flames burning. This young intern taught me how biased I am. My generation of pastors is a product of revival. We see ourselves as keepers of the fire. The Jesus Movement is long past, but our churches continue to prosper in its wake. However, that revival belongs to the Baby Boom, a rising tide of middle-aged people. Authors are already recording and even revising the history of what really happened in the early 1970s. Two more generations are on the horizon. One is just coming into adolescence. The other is in early adulthood and hurting in every way possible.[113]

I live in the easy chair of mid-life success. I've been privileged to help birth scores of *daughter* and *granddaughter* congregations. Our church is replete with people in ministry. Many of them look forward to planting a church. I teach others about raising leadership and launching ministry. My adult children Carl and Kelly have already helped pioneer two churches. Put in other terms, "I am happy." Because of all the blessings in my life, I have a serious interest in the *status quo.* These gifts from God now stand in the way of any fresh approach to ministry on my part. If I don't initiate it or at least feel a strong emotional bond with it, it isn't going to happen in my vicinity.

Me, a Hindrance?

I wonder if I could become (or presently am) a hindrance to revival and awakening. My admitted problem is that my understanding of truth is sculptured by my experience. I must admit that God is bigger than my understanding and that His ways are higher than my experience, if I expect to participate in the next revival.

It is not enough to relish the size of what we have. I must admit the spiritual poverty that leaves the whitened fields largely unharvested. We simply lose the battle if we pride ourselves in our accomplishments without acknowledging the need and opportunity around us. I've stopped measuring the size of our church against others in the community. I now measure it against the size of the unchurched population within driving distance. This is humbling that the unchurched population contains people ravaged by drugs, perverted sex, and violence. Jesus died for them. I must love them. I must reach them. I don't have to think like them to reach them. But someone around me must. In teaching, the language must be common to teachers and leaders. I must admit that I don't speak their language and that I must make room for someone who does. The next *Ralph Moore* in my church probably watches MTV and wears oversized pants pulled tightly around his waist by a black belt with a huge buckle. He probably respects me but thinks I couldn't appreciate his youth or his culture. I might find him a little brash and be turned off by his computer games or his haircut. He probably comes from a single-parent family and may even be a welfare child. He also communicates well with his generation. I do not.

We're Both Needy

This person needs me and I need him. He needs my endorsement and wisdom. I need him as a vessel to hold the wisdom passed to me from men who have gone before. He becomes the keeper of all that I hold dear. He is also a spark God will use to bring impact to his generation as I am to mine.

The all important question is, "Will I even recognize him?" Is this person sitting in my congregation right now? Is he or she a part of my own family? Are he and his friends turned off by our ministry? Are they on the way out the door because we aren't sensitive to their needs? Is this the person we just had to discipline and are now trying to disciple?

These are more than interesting questions. They lay the base for any future ministry I will have. I intend to influence the world through my middle years and into old age, perhaps, even from beyond the grave. The only way I can do this is by fanning the small fires of revival in the hearts of people who may make me feel a little uncomfortable.

Final Options

Like you, I want to hear those words, "Well done good and faithful servant." Faithfulness to today's task may feel like betrayal of my own past. But my past experiences are not the point, expansion of God's Kingdom is. The harvest is whiter than ever, the laborers look younger every day. If my kernel of wheat needs to fall into the ground in order to bring on a new harvest, so be it. I am ready to sacrifice the comfortable for something new, if unnerving. What about you? Are you willing to pay the price to have your prayers answered?

Endnotes

1. II Chronicles 7:14.
2. J. Edwin Orr, *Campus Aflame: A History of Evangelical Awakenings in Collegiate Communities* (Wheaton, IL: International Awakening Press), p. 161, 162.
3. John Naisbitt, *Megatrends 2000* (New York: William Morrow, 1990), p. 295–296.
4. William Strauss and Neil Howe, *Generations: The History of America's Future, 1584 to 2069* (New York: Quill-William Morrow, 1991), p. 124.
5. Ibid., p. 132.
6. Ibid., p. 129.
7. Ibid., pp. 133–134.
8. Cotton Mather, *Magnalia Christi Americana, Book II,* as quoted by Peter Marshall and David Manuel, *The Light and the Glory* (Grand Rapids: Fleming H. Revell, 1977), p. 216.
9. Ibid., pp. 219–220.
10. Psalm 45:17.
11. I Peter 2:9 (KJV).
12. Proverbs 30:11–14 (KJV).
13. Matthew 12:45 (KJV).
14. Hebrews 3:10–13.
15. Jeremiah 7:29.
16. Acts 2:40.
17. Ecclesiastes 1:4.

18. George Barna, *Virtual America: What Every Church Leader Needs to Know About Ministering in an Age of Spiritual and Technological Revolution* (Ventura, CA: Regal Books, 1994), p. 47.
19. Ibid., p. 85.
20. Ibid., pp. 111–112.
21. Strauss and Howe, p. 317.
22. Barna, *Virtual America*, p. 69.
23. Strauss and Howe, pp. 208–209.
24. *America's Great Revivals* (Minneapolis: Dimension Books, Bethany Fellowship), pp. 18–20.
25. Peter Marshall and David Manuel, *From Sea to Shining Sea* (Grand Rapids: Fleming H. Revell, 1986), pp. 62–62, 102.
26. Acts 10:47–48.
27. Acts 11:17–18.
28. Acts 12:19.
29. Acts 18:22.
30. Proverbs 13:22; Joel 1:3.
31. Alfred F. Kuen, *I Will Build My Church* (Chicago: Moody Press, 1971), pp. 227–233.
32. Hoito Edoin, *The Night Tokyo Burned: The Incendiary Campaign Against Japan*, March–August 1945 (New York: St. Martin's Press, 1987), pp. 34–39.
33. Acts 2:2.
34. Acts 2:3.
35. F.F. Bruce, *The Spreading Flame: The Rise and Progress of Christianity From Its First Beginnings to the Conversion of the English* (Grand Rapids: William B. Eerdmans Publishing Co., 1958), pp. 286–288.
36. Acts 8:1.
37. Acts 8:1–8, 14.
38. Acts 11:19–26.
39. Acts 1:8.
40. George Barna, *Evangelism That Works* (Ventura, CA: Regal Books, 1995), pp. 113–116.
41. C. Peter Wagner, "Who Found It?" *Eternity Magazine*, September 1977, pp. 13–19.
42. Winfield C. Arn, "Mass Evangelism: The Bottom Line," *Church Growth America*, January–February 1978, p. 7.
43. C. Peter Wagner, *Church Planting for a Greater Harvest* (Ventura, CA: Regal Books, 1990), p. 12.
44. Ibid., p. 32.
45. Arn, p. 7.
46. Wagner, "Who Found It?" pp. 13–19.

47. "You Win Some, You Lose More: Indecent Proposals," *Ministry Currents,* July–September 1993, p. 14.
48. George Barna, *The Barna Report, 1992–1993* (Ventura, CA: Regal Books, 1993), pp. 102, 283.
49. Matthew 28:19.
50. Ephesians 4:12.
51. Robert Lacey, *Ford: The Men and the Machine* (New York: Ballentine Books, 1986), pp. 320–321.
52. Lyle E. Schaller, *It's a Different World* (Nashville: Abingdon Press, 1987), p. 198.
53. Ibid., pp. 200–211.
54. Lyle E. Schaller, *The Senior Minister* (Nashville: Abingdon Press, 1990), pp. 84–85.
55. Kenneth B. Mulholland, *Adventures in Training the Ministry: A Honduran Case Study in Theological Education by Extension* (Nutley, NJ: Presbyterian and Reformed Publishing Co., 1976), pp. 9–10.
56. Ibid., pp. 4–5.
57. Ibid., p. 8.
58. John Dillenberger and Claude Welch, *Protestant Christianity Interpreted Through Its Development* (New York: Charles Scribner's Sons, 1954), p. 148.
59. Edwin Scott Gaustad, *Historical Atlas of Religion in America* (New York: Harper and Row, 1962), p. 55.
60. Neil Braun, *Laity Mobilized: Reflections on Church Growth in Japan and Other Lands* (Grand Rapids: William B. Eerdmans Publishing Co., 1971), p. 55.
61. Otis Cary, *Protestant Missions,* Vol. II of *A History of Christianity in Japan* (Tokyo: Charles E. Tuttle Company, 1976), pp. 163, 296.
62. Author's observations of Japanese Christian movements include: (1) Shalom churches under Pastor Elmer Inafuku with 10 large congregations in 22 years; (2) New Life churches led by Pastor Akihiro Mizuno with 19 congregations in the same time frame, using the same principles. Pastor David Masui of Hakodate Zion Kyokai has used this method to raise pastors and plant churches in his own and other church families.
63. Cary, pp. 171, 320.
64. Total Sports, http://www.totalbaseball.com/story/event/record/lifetime/atl1c9.htm.
65. Acts 14:22–23.
66. Acts 17:1–10.
67. Acts 14:23.
68. *The Kiplinger Washington Letter,* Vol. 74, No. 1, January 3, 1997.

69. Andy Crouch, "A Generation of Debtors," *Christianity Today*, November 11, 1996, pp. 31–32.
70. "Generation X-onomics," *The Economist*, March 19, 1994.
71. Ibid.
72. Ibid.
73. Lynn Marian, "Generation X: Reaching Tomorrow's Customers Today," *Christian Retailing*, June 10, 1996, p. 58.
74. Randall Lane, "Computers Are Our Friends," *Forbes*, May 8, 1995, p. 102.
75. Marian, p. 58.
76. Lane, p. 102.
77. Psalm 78:2.
78. John 15:1-4.
79. Staff of Leadership Network, "alt.ministry@genX.forum," *NEXT Magazine* (Vol. 2, No. 7, April 1996).
80. Steve Rabey, "Pastor X," *Christianity Today*, November 11, 1996, pp. 40–43.
81. Marian, "Generation X," pp. 58–59.
82. Marian, "Swing Poll," *Swing Magazine*, April 1996, p. 59.
83. Crouch, p. 32.
84. Bob Whitesell, "News That Impacts Your Ministry," *Strategies for Today's Leader*, Vol. XXXIII, No. 3, pp. 26–29.
85. Lane, p. 105.
86. Whitesell, p. 28.
87. Marian, p. 58.
88. Lane, p. 104.
89. Bob Buford, *Half Time* (Grand Rapids: Zondervan Publishing House, 1994), pp. 88–89.
90. Bruce Tulgan, *Managing Generation X: How to Bring Out the Best in Young Talent* (Santa Monica, CA: Merritt Publishing, 1995).
91. Staff of Leadership Network.
92. David Goetz, "The Church's Ten-Year Window," *Leadership Journal*, Winter 1997.
93. Mark 4:34.
94. George Barna, *Evangelism That Works* (Ventura, CA: Regal Books, 1995), pp. 113–115.
95. Whitesell, pp. 26–29.
96. Ibid., p. 26.
97. I Corinthians 14:26.
98. Charles Truehart, "Welcome to the Next Church," *The Atlantic Monthly*, August 1996, pp. 37–58.

99. "Labor Shortages Are Spreading," *The Kiplinger Washington Newsletter,* Vol. 74, No. 4, January 24, 1997.
100. Lane, p. 102.
101. Staff of Leadership Network, pp. 2-3.
102. II Corinthians 14:26.
103. Truehart, p. 37.
104. Leighton Ford, "A Letter to Future Leaders," *Christianity Today,* November 11, 1996.
105. Matthew 22:37-39.
106. William Shaw, "Jesus Rocks but Does He Mosh?" *Details Magazine,* October 1996, p. 76.
107. Chuck and Gina Reischman, "Reaching Generation X and Beyond," *Spread the Fire Magazine,* November/December 1996, http://www.tacf.org/stf/1-6/article1/html.
108. I Corinthians 9:22.
109. Barna, *Evangelism That Works,* pp. 113-115.
110. I Corinthians 5:10-12.
111. Ford.
112. Ralph Moore and Daniel T. Beach, *Let Go of the Ring: The Hope Chapel Story* (Honolulu: Straight Street Publishing, 1993).
113. Strauss and Howe, pp. 317-324.

Ralph Moore

can be heard on "Word of Hope" every weekday
on KLHT, 1040 AM, at 5:30 p.m.
and on KAIM, 95.5 FM at 9 p.m.
Hawaii

Hope Chapel Kaneohe
Oahu • Hawaii

hope@aloha.net
www.hopechapel.com

Other Resources

STRAIGHT STREET PUBLISHING

A ministry of Hope Chapel Kaneohe

■

P.O. Box 240041
Honolulu, HI 96824-0041

■

1-800-711-9369 or 1-808-235-5814
Email: hope@aloha.net
Website: www.hopechapel.com

On a "street called Straight,"
scales fell from the eyes of Saul of Tarsus.
It was there that he began to see
the way that led to establishing
the Church in new territories.
It is our goal to stir your thought
and increase your vision
for expanding the Church into all the nations.

Discovering Minichurch: Small Groups That Really Work

by Ralph Moore • only $69.95

Includes six audio cassettes and 41-page workbook. This dynamic series will provide the tools required to meet the expectations and demands of today's church and the future. With practical, proven techniques, *Discovering MiniChurch* will help you lead your congregation to a deeper understanding and commitment in their relationship with Christ. You'll also receive pastoral tools that will not only increase your effectiveness, but ease the tremendous burdens you face as a leader of your ministry.

Discovering Advanced Church Planting

by Ralph Moore • only $89.95

Includes eight audio cassettes and 54-page workbook. In this breakthrough training series, Ralph Moore will not only provide you with the "nuts and bolts" of church planting, but will also give you the not-so-obvious insights that comes from a seasoned and experienced "church planter." He'll take you beyond the step-by-step approach most church planting resources provide and guide you through the difficult relational issues all church planters have to deal with. *Discovering Advanced Church Planting* provides a wealth of information and wisdom that could save you months of frustration.

Let Go of the Ring
by Ralph Moore
$13.95

Letting go is difficult, but it is the only way to success. This 200-plus page book chronicles the story of Hope Chapel and Ralph Moore's struggle to give God the "ultimate authority" in his life. And how, when he finally "let go of the ring," his ministry was so greatly blessed.

Choices
by Ralph Moore
$10.95

God does love you and has a wonderful plan for your life! This book will help you understand that God's plan is available to you. You will discover that God has given you a "manual," describing His will for your life. You will also find that He has given you the freedom to make CHOICES.

Financial Freedom
by Ralph Moore
$10.95

In this book Ralph offers a simple, readable, and honest plan for financial success. Hundreds of young families at Hope Chapel can testify to the simple practicality of his teaching. Learn how to bring yourself into partnership with God and His promise to meet your financial needs.

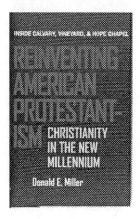

Reinventing American Protestantism
by Donald E. Miller
$27.50

Drawing on more than five years of research and hundreds of interviews, this book takes us inside "new paradigm churches" and explores three of the movements that have created them: Calvary Chapel, Vineyard Christian Fellowship, and Hope Chapel. Miller argues that these churches are involved in a second Reformation that seeks to challenge mainstream Christian worship.

Why Believe?
by Kelly Michael Hilderbrand
$10.95

An excellent tool for a new believer's class, new member's class, or everyday witnessing. Written for the Christian and non-Christian alike, this book provides authoritative answers to common questions and misconceptions about Christianity, along with hope for a more meaningful life through a personal relationship with God.

Just Another Lump of Clay
by Michael Bagby
$13.95

From the cockpit of the Navy's A-6 Intruder to the slopes of Vail, Colorado, to the jungles of Central America . . . this is the true story of the transformation of one man seeking the true meaning of life. Through his inspirational and faith-building autobiography, Michael shares powerful testimony about God's faithfulness and provisions.

Order Form

 Phone (Mon–Fri, 9AM–5PM Hawaii)
(800) 711-9369 toll-free
(808) 235-5814

Website: www.hopechapel.com

🖥 **Email order to:**
hope@aloha.net

Mail order form to:
Straight Street Publishing
P.O. Box 240041
Honolulu, HI 96824-0041

 Fax order form to:
(808) 247-2070

(PLEASE PRINT)

MR/MRS/MS FIRST	LAST
CHURCH/ORGANIZATION	DENOMINATION
MAILING ADDRESS	

CITY	STATE	ZIP CODE / ZIP+4

PHONE NO. ( )	FAX NO. ( )	EMAIL ADDRESS

TITLE AND DESCRIPTION	PRICE EACH	QTY.	TOTAL PRICE
Let Go of the Ring, 3rd Ed. (book)	$13.95		

PAYMENT (All orders must be prepaid):

____ Check   ____ Money Order

Please make check/money order payable to:
Straight Street Publishing

____ VISA
____ MasterCard   Expiration Date: _____

SUBTOTAL	
SHIPPING (See chart below)	
TOTAL	

CREDIT CARD NO.

CARDHOLDER'S NAME (please print)

SIGNATURE

SHIPPING
Via Air Mail U.S. Postal Service

If SUBTOTAL is:
Up to $20.00, add $3.00 to order;
$20.01–$50.00, please add $4.00;
Over $50.00, add 8% of SUBTOTAL.

Thank you for your order.